PEOPLE THAT CHANGED THE COURSE OF HISTORY

THE STORY OF

FRANK LLOYD WRIGHT

150 YEARS
AFTER HIS BIRTH

HANNAH M. SANDOVAL

1405 SW 6th Avenue • Ocala, Florida 34471 • Phone 800-814-1132 • Fax 352-622-1875
Web site: www.atlantic-pub.com • E-mail: sales@atlantic-pub.com
SAN Number: 268-1250

Library of Congress Cataloging-in-Publication Data

Names: Sandoval, Hannah M., 1993-
Title: People that changed the course of history : the story of Frank Lloyd
   Wright 150 years after his birth / Hannah M. Sandoval.
Description: Ocala, Florida : Atlantic Publishing Group, Inc., 2017. |
   Includes bibliographical references and index.
Identifiers: LCCN 2016049057 (print) | LCCN 2016050625 (ebook) | ISBN
   9781620231470 (alk. paper) | ISBN 1620231476 (alk. paper) | ISBN
   9781620231548 (ebook)
Subjects: LCSH: Wright, Frank Lloyd, 1867-1959--Biography. |
   Architects--United States--Biography.
Classification: LCC NA737.W7 S285 2017 (print) | LCC NA737.W7 (ebook) | DDC
   720.92 [B] --dc23
LC record available at https://lccn.loc.gov/2016049057

PROJECT MANAGER: Rebekah Sack • rsack@atlantic-pub.com
ASSISTANT EDITOR: Rebekah Slonim • rebekah.slonim@gmail.com
INTERIOR LAYOUT: Steven W. Booth • steven@geniusbookcompany.com
COVER DESIGN: Jackie Miller • millerjackiej@gmail.com
JACKET DESIGN: Steven W. Booth • steven@geniusbookcompany.com

Printed in the United States

Reduce. Reuse.
RECYCLE.

A decade ago, Atlantic Publishing signed the Green Press Initiative. These guidelines promote environmentally friendly practices, such as using recycled stock and vegetable-based inks, avoiding waste, choosing energy-efficient resources, and promoting a no-pulping policy. We now use 100-percent recycled stock on all our books. The results: in one year, switching to post-consumer recycled stock saved 24 mature trees, 5,000 gallons of water, the equivalent of the total energy used for one home in a year, and the equivalent of the greenhouse gases from one car driven for a year.

Over the years, we have adopted a number of dogs from rescues and shelters. First there was Bear and after he passed, Ginger and Scout. Now, we have Kira, another rescue. They have brought immense joy and love not just into our lives, but into the lives of all who met them.

We want you to know a portion of the profits of this book will be donated in Bear, Ginger and Scout's memory to local animal shelters, parks, conservation organizations, and other individuals and nonprofit organizations in need of assistance.

– Douglas & Sherri Brown,
President & Vice-President of Atlantic Publishing

Table of Contents

Introduction

Young Frank Lloyd Wright's mink-collared coat and bowtie drew unusual looks from passerby as he took a leisurely stroll by the Wisconsin State Capitol building. The sounds of hammers and working men calling to each other met his ears as he passed the new north wing that was still under construction.

Frank jumped back in alarm as an earth-shaking roar issued from the big, white, partially finished dome. From a safe distance, Frank watched in horror as the dome collapsed in a massive cloud of white limestone that swirled in the air and then settled in a chalky film over the surrounding trees, buildings, and people. When the dust cleared, Frank wished it hadn't, for it had blocked the grisly sights of death and destruction. He saw working men covered head to foot in limestone fleeing for their lives as huge stone chunks, heavy beams, and other still-falling debris crashed down on top of them. He saw many men die under the weight. He watched helplessly as a man pinned by an iron beam in a window 50 feet up moaned, "Help me, please!"

His heart pounding and his stomach queasy, Frank couldn't pull himself away, as much as he wanted to. The firemen came first. Next, crowds of good Samaritans rushed to try to pull the wreckage off the surviving workers. Then came the family members of the fallen. Frank clung, ashen-faced, to an iron fence surrounding the park nearby, unable to tear his eyes away as tear-streaked mothers, daughters, sisters, and wives began to move slowly through the chalky white bricks and iron beams looking for their loved ones.

At last, after hours of stupefied, frozen observance, Frank went home sick to his stomach. Frank was an aspiring architect, and he was living and working at the University of Wisconsin and taking classes on engineering (the closest thing he could find to architecture classes in the area). He went to bed wondering how a building by such a good architect could have caused such destruction. He had nightmares for days.

A few days later, Frank read in the paper that the architect had built concrete piers in the building's basement to hold up the columns that supported the whole building. However, the architect hadn't overseen the full installment of these piers. He hadn't been there when the contractor had tried to cut corners by filling those piers with broken bits of brick and stone as a support system, rather than filling them with concrete or something else reliable. Frank was alarmed to find out, though, that it was the architect — not the contractor — who would be charged with manslaughter.

Sitting on his bed at the University, newspaper in hand, Frank decided that when he became an architect (for there was no doubt in his young mind that he *would* be an architect — and a great one at that) he would make sure all of his buildings were made with solid, safe materials. He would see to it himself.

Chapter 1
Frank, The Boy

Frank Lloyd Wright was born just after the Civil War ended. As a child, his family would have gotten around with a horse and buggy. By the time he died at the start of the Space Age, cars were a commonplace item and man had built rockets to launch themselves into space! So much changed in his lifetime, and yet, he remained relevant, well-known, and admired right up until the day he died. So how did he manage to create architecture that's considered true American art? How did he become the father of modernism? Let's start at the beginning and find out.

Humble Beginnings

Frank Lloyd Wright's life has always been shrouded in myth and legend, much of it woven by Frank himself. Even his birthdate remained something of a mystery for a while. Born on June 8, 1867 in Richland Center, Wisconsin, he later began telling people he was born in 1869 in order to seem younger and to make his success more impressive.

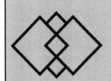 *Fast Fact:* In reality, Frank's sister Jane was born in 1869, and truth be told, she didn't appreciate having her birth year stolen from her.

His name wasn't always Frank Lloyd Wright, either. He was born Frank Lincoln Wright. His mother strongly supported President Lincoln and his anti-slavery movement, so she initially named her son after him. Later,

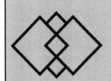

though, Frank's middle name was changed to honor his mother's Welsh immigrant family, the Lloyd Joneses. This name change signified a shift in his loyalty that reflected the turmoil of his early home life.

Frank and his two sisters, Jane and Maginel, were born to Anna Lloyd

Jones and William Russell Cary Wright. Frank was a small boy, only growing to 5'7" (though he often wore heeled boots to hide it), but he showed big talent from an early age. He inherited a talent for music from his father. He loved the piano most of all.[1]

It could be said that Frank's parents married more out of mutual necessity rather than true love. Anna was approaching 30, and back in those times, that meant she was soon to be known as what's called a spinster — meaning she would be too old to marry and would have to live alone or with her family. William already had three children from his deceased first wife, and he needed somebody to help care for them.

Things started out great. Anna was a highly educated Welsh immigrant with big hopes who was eager to start a family.

What did Anna Lloyd Jones look like? Frank Lloyd Wright's mother has been described by many (including Frank himself) as strong and dark, from her long brown hair to her strong brow to her captivating dark eyes beneath. She walked with the confidence of a man, and though she strove to uphold her family's values of grace and stoicism, she was a spitfire who let her passions pull her in all directions.

William caught her attention because he was charming and intelligent (two traits he passed on to Frank). He knew how to speak and how to make people fall in love with him. As a result, he had no trouble finding work as a preacher. Getting paid for it was the problem. The economy was in bad shape in the 1870s, and William often went unpaid. When he was paid, it was often through organized donations from the congregation, and nobody seemed to give much. William also taught music and had passed the bar exam to become a lawyer, but despite all of his talent, he just couldn't seem to make ends meet. The family had to move around a lot, finding new places for William to work until the money dried up there, too.

Anna didn't like having to leave her large, tight-knit family in Wisconsin. She didn't like wasting away in poverty. She was educated and wild; she needed more freedom. Anna's homesickness and William's financial struggles put a strain on the marriage. It became harder and harder to support their large family of eight.

Frank lived in poverty, but thanks to his mother, he went to a fashionable school and soaked up all the latest teachings. Anna managed to send Frank — and only Frank — to a private school, where Frank was surrounded by rich boys whom he called the "Snobbyists and the Goodyites" in his autobiography.[2] It's not surprising that his childhood best friend went to one of two Madison ward schools rather than Frank's private school.

Frank, who would later be known for his arrogance, met his childhood best friend, Robie Lamp, through a moment of heroic empathy.

What did Robie Lamp look like? Frank's best friend, Robie, was a kind boy with flaming hair and crystal blue eyes; he was crippled from the waist down and had to use crutches to get around.

Though his chest and arm muscles were extraordinarily strong, a large group of schoolboys had snatched away Robie's crutches and were burying him in a pile of autumn leaves. Frank, usually a loner who kept to himself, ran off the other boys, retrieved Robie's crutches, and made an instant life-long friend.[3] Robie was a boy after Frank's own heart. He loved music, and he loved inventing things. Robie took violin lessons from Frank's father, and the two spent nearly every day together, playing music, inventing, designing, reading, and having childhood adventures. Often at Frank's house.

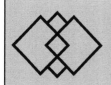 **Fast Fact: During their childhood romps, Robie and Frank built a cross-gun, a bob-sled, and a sort of paddle boat they dubbed the Frankenrob.**[4]

Frank came home from his fancy school every day to a plain house. Anna believed in simple, elegant decoration — perhaps because the family's meager means wouldn't allow anything else. She never trimmed her picked flowers and never arranged them in elaborate designs. Instead, she liked to put just a few in each vase so that you could see the stems and petals of each individually. She believed in plain cooking, making her stews and potatoes and meats without any sauces or fancy seasonings. Frank resented not being able to have some of the finer things in life. He couldn't have pie or cake or store-bought candy. Instead, his mother gave him gingerbread and molasses candy.[5]

Though he may have resented being denied fancy desserts, his mother's plain, natural approach to design and decoration stuck with Frank and can be seen in his own work. This was just one of the ways his mother would prove to be the main driving influence behind his extraordinary life and success.

Life on the Farm

When it became clear that moving from town to town wasn't actually improving their financial issues, the family moved back to Wisconsin. Anna called on her large family for support. Her brothers and uncles looked down on Frank's father, William, for not being able to support his family. Frank grew up observing their disapproving stares. Despite the countless attributes he shared with his father, Frank began to turn to the men in his mother's family for his life examples — their strong work ethics and their conservative morals.

Frank loved to draw, read, and play piano. All of these activities kept him indoors. He was a highly independent child, and he didn't get out or play with others (besides Robie Lamp) very much. This concerned his mother, and she sent him to work on her family's farm in The Valley when he turned 11.

Farm work is no picnic, and Frank absolutely hated it. He hated it so much, in fact, that he tried to run away more than once, but never got very far. He had to wake up before the sun, awoken roughly by his Uncle James pounding on a stove pipe that heated his room. He had to milk and feed the cows. He had to carry lumber and help build fences.

As much as Frank despised this hard, sweaty farm business, it taught him the value of hard work — to keep working until one is sore, working until one grows stronger for it. It taught him to do things with his hands. Most importantly, it connected him to nature. He would walk among the lush landscape of the valley, observing the trees. It was nature's beauty that he strove to recreate in his own personal style of architecture, emulating the magnificence of what he saw around him.

A spring ran by the farmhouse, and Frank loved to play in it. His play wasn't just splashing around, either. No, not Frank. Frank liked to build dams out of sticks and stones. He liked to use his shoes as boats and watch them float downstream. He developed a fascination with running water.

He often had to go into the woods to fetch the wandering cows, and he took his time there. He liked to observe the birds and all their different colors. He liked to memorize the trees. He worked from before sunrise to sunset, and he took in all the brilliance and colors of both. He would run off into the woods barefoot with the huge sky overhead, and no matter how many times his uncles and aunts tried to call him back, they couldn't keep him from taking in the colors and majesty of the forest.

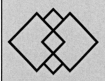

Fast Fact: When Frank was older, he signed all of his architectural drawings with a little red square. According to Frank, it was a reminder of a sublime experience he had on the Wisconsin prairie. He looked down while walking through a green field and saw a red tiger lily. The beauty of the bright, fierce red on the gentle green transfixed him. He never forgot it or the way it made him feel.

A Mother's Plan

Despite his free-spirited, transcendent romps in the forest, Frank certainly didn't grow up in a fairytale. He grew up in real poverty, and he witnessed the turmoil between his parents at a very young age. Anna became something of a wicked step mother to William's three children from his previous marriage. (Maybe it was like a fairytale after all?) According to court records filed during Anna and William's eventual divorce, Anna was abusive to William and his children, and she was prone to wild, violent fits of rage.[6] It was so bad that William eventually sent his children away to live with other relatives.

But Frank was different. Frank was special. To Anna, he could do no wrong, and she treated him like a golden boy — an angel. She neglected not only William and his children in favor of Frank, but her own two daughters as well. She doted on him with an almost obsessively fierce passion. When she sent him to the farm, she cried as she cut off his long curls to give him a haircut better suited for hard labor.[7] She cried again when she dropped him off. She did not want to give up his youth in the form of those curls and accept that he was getting older. She certainly didn't want to leave him in a new place, away from her. More than anything, though, she was determined to give her boy everything he needed to become great, and she saw life on the farm as another way to do so.

From even before he was born, she decided he would be an architect. She did everything she could to influence him to take up that dream. Frank himself recalls pictures of beautiful English Cathedrals being framed on the walls by his crib. Against the odds, Anna got him a few years of private schooling. She herself was a teacher, and she spent her days with her precious boy, teaching him all she knew. In Anna's mind, Frank was her way out of a life of poverty. She just knew he was destined for greatness.

As a result of her never-ending adoration of him, Frank grew to idolize his mother. While others might have described her as unstable, he saw her as high spirited. He blamed his father for all the troubles at home, believing that William was simply jealous of Anna's devotion to Frank over him.

Frank grew up to be a bit of a "bad boy," despite spending every Sunday in his mother's family's strict, conservative church. He was like the member of a boy band group who starts a solo career, trades in bubblegum pop for something "edgier," gets a big head, and then starts to show up in the tabloids for all kinds of scandals. Although … maybe that's not quite right. Frank had his fair share of scandals, for certain, but he definitely never had screaming fans idolizing and adoring him — at least not in his youth. No, he was ahead of his time, and his art was not understood at first. It was too futuristic, too out-of-the-box, too bizarre.

Still, despite his shortcomings and despite how far he eventually strayed from his family's roots, his mother was always there. No matter how many other women came into his life, Anna always took care of him and made excuses for him when he slipped up. More importantly, she pushed him to be the best he could be. She gave him self-confidence (perhaps a little too much). She gave him all of the resources she could afford. Her dedication paid off in a big way, maybe even more so than she'd imagined.

Sources

1   Huxtable, 2004.

2   Wright, 1977.

3   Wright, 1977.

4   Wright, 1977.

5   Wright, 1977.

6   Huxtable, 2004.

7   Wright, 1977.

Chapter 2
An Architect at Heart

Friedrich Froebel

In 1876, when Frank was about nine, Anna attended the Centennial Exposition in Philadelphia. It was the first World's Fair and was held in honor of the 100th anniversary of America's independence. It's really no surprise that she came back from that event bearing a special gift for Frank. Gifts, in fact. The Friedrich Froebel gifts.

Mr. Friedrich Froebel was a famous German teacher. His self-titled "gifts" were a lot like the building blocks and construction paper that just about every child plays with at some point in his or her life these days. Anna came home with her arms full of pegs, wooden blocks of all shapes (cubes, pyramids, cylinders, spheres), and colorful paper. The toys were meant for advanced kindergarten teaching, but Anna was thinking back to those English Cathedrals she framed above Frank's crib.[1] These were the perfect toys for her little architect. These could teach him that all those grand buildings started out as basic geometric shapes. All one had to do to create architectural masterpieces was put them together in the right way.

These toys weren't meant for babies; kindergarten didn't always mean school for toddlers. Froebel intended his gifts to be used by older children, too. Frank took to them instantly. He rolled them over in his hands, studying their texture and form. He became fascinated by — maybe even addicted to — the shapes he could make from them. The bright colors, so like those birds and flowers he would come to love in the fields and woods beside his grandparents' farm house, captivated him.

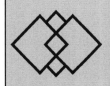

Fast Fact: Friedrich Froebel is often hailed as The Father of Kindergarten. The word kindergarten is German for "children's playground." Froebel's gifts were the special toys meant for the children in this "playground."

Delighted with how well Frank took to the gifts, Anna managed to hunt down and get her hands on the next set in the series called the occupations. The occupations included more advanced lessons meant to help children seek out and experiment with geometric form. Anna, a teacher, became an expert in Froebel's teaching methods, traveling all the way to Boston to learn from another teacher. Near the end of the day, when she was done with cleaning and cooking and all her other daily chores, she would sit with Frank for long periods of time each day until he became an expert, too.

Some historians and researchers have theorized that Frank's love of including triangles and pinwheels in his architecture traces back to those early lessons with his mother and those special toys. Indeed, Frank himself credited Froebel's gifts and occupations with spawning the geometric forms in his work.

The truth of this is evidenced by the appearance of crystallography in his work. Crystallography studies the shapes that atoms make inside crystals. Many of Frank's designs included hexagonal chains that mimicked the way atoms come together to make crystals. He used mirror imagery in his work: making buildings that were perfectly symmetrical and identical when split down the middle. The atoms in crystals often form mirror images.

But why did Frank use crystallography in his work? What does that have to do with Froebel's special toys? Well, Froebel was a crystallographer before he decided to become a teacher, and he based his toys on crystallography.

It seems that Frank never let go of Froebel's influence, bestowed upon him early in life by his ever-doting mother.

Nature's Architecture

Frank grew up amid the romanticism of the end of the 19th century, when people were casting off the thinking of the Age of Enlightenment: a period where people believed that meaning and truth only came through rational thought. This was not a very imaginative worldview, and Frank was an imaginative boy. He embraced the romantic ideas of people like Ralph Waldo Emerson who said that true enlightenment and knowledge come from finding a "oneness" with nature. His mother, of course, was the one to read him romantic poems and somehow, despite her lack of funds, she acquired books by people like Thoreau and Emerson for him.[2]

Frank eventually came to identify with the transcendentalists, a more extreme version of the romantics, headed by people like William Wordsworth and Walt Whitman. Transcendentalists worshipped nature as a divine teacher from which ultimate truth could be obtained. They rejected everything artificial, from industry to traditional classroom-based teaching methods. Anna read him poems that reflected this idea, and Frank soaked them up, learning to look to nature for answers and for beauty.

When he grew older and began crafting his famous buildings, he dubbed his work "organic architecture." He let the lay of the land dictate the structure and design of the building instead of forcing the land to fit a prefabricated vision for the building. In his mind, his work created a unity between nature, the universe, and his own spirit.

He never abandoned these romantic beliefs. He never stopped trying to create unity with nature through his work. Even the industrial age and all its technological advancements and influences couldn't sway him. It's probably why his work was so unique — so "out there." His architectural creations always seemed to fit perfectly within the landscape on which he chose to build, as if they sprouted, took root, and grew from the earth itself.

The Day the Music Stopped

Frank's relationship with his father, William, was complicated. In his early childhood, his father was a figure of awe. Watching his father speak eloquently in front of the congregation on Sundays made Frank proud. Frank also admired his father's musical talent. In fact, music was the one thing that connected the two, but even those memories were not always pleasant. When William would play the church organ, he would have Frank man the bellows in the dark back room to keep the organ playing. To keep the pressure just right, Frank had to use a wooden lever to release some of the air. William often got lost in playing Bach and forgot about his small son pumping away at that lever until he couldn't possibly pump anymore.[3]

Still, William didn't only make Frank help him play music; he taught Frank to play himself — violin and piano. William gave Frank one of his greatest passions, and throughout his life, Frank would remember his father in relation to music — his passion as he played, the ink smeared on his face and hands as he composed his own songs, and the gentle way he spoke when teaching Frank and the other schoolchildren in his music class how to play together.

It seemed, though, that Frank always came between his parents without intending to, making the rift created by their financial situation greater. When William brought Frank home, exhausted from pumping the organ bellows, Anna became angry with William. When Anna gave Frank preferential treatment over William and the other children, William became angry with Anna.

Caught in the middle of an escalating war between his parents, Frank chose a side: his mother's.[4] He never talked about her violent rages. He always made her out to be a sort of saint. Perhaps the ugly side of Anna never really impressed on him because he was always spared it. He was the golden boy, and his mother did nothing but adore him.

Frank never formed a strong bond with his father. Anna was ever-present, hovering over him, but William retreated into himself. Ashamed by his failures and beaten down by his wife's anger, he kept to himself and his music.

The truth of Anna's instability only came out when historians began digging into Frank's life after his death to try and uncover the true man behind all of the legends and myths. Those historians found the court documents for Anna and William's ugly divorce.

William was the one to file for divorce, stating that his wife showed him no love, neglected him, and violently abused him when he could not give her the things she wanted. Anna is cited in the court records as stating that she did, in fact, have no love for him,[5] and the court decided that William's claims were valid and approved the divorce.

Anna's family, the Lloyd Joneses, unsurprisingly took Anna's side. They were sick of Anna and her children living in poverty. They didn't want William around anymore. They told William that if he would just leave them all alone, they would support Anna and her three children.

At this point, William was even farther down on his luck than usual. Nobody wanted to take music lessons from him anymore; it's also possible that they simply couldn't afford to. When the family had moved back to Wisconsin, William had converted from Baptist to Unitarianism (the denomination of Anna's family), but he wasn't making much money as a Unitarian preacher either. Down on his luck and unable to support his family, William didn't really have a choice but to comply with the Lloyd Jones' request if he wanted what was best for his family.

So, William obliged and left with nothing but his violin and his clothes. Anna got the house and everything else, and Frank, then 18, never saw his father again. Frank didn't even attend his funeral.[6] He quit studying music when his father left and didn't pick it back up in college. Architecture was his focus now — fulfilling his mother's vision, not his father's.

Though the official court accounts make it clear that Anna was the one to push William away and then eventually cast him out, Frank held to the fiction created by Anna that William abandoned them for his whole life. Perhaps the truth was too painful. Why hold onto the man who was no longer around (and who had hardly been "present" when he was around), when he still had his mother to rely on? So, he adopted her story and followed her well-laid plan for him, but he never forgot the image of his father with ink on his face and hands or the sound of Bach pouring from the keys beneath his father's fingers.

Sources

1   Huxtable, 2004.

2   Huxtable, 2004.

3   Wright, 1977.

4   Huxtable, 2004.

5   Huxtable, 2004.

6   Huxtable, 2004.

Chapter 3
A Rising Star

It appears that Frank never actually finished high school, and the grades he did get were less than stellar. Anna was met with a new dilemma. William was gone, so there was even less money than usual. More importantly, there weren't any schools that taught architecture in the Midwest, and she definitely couldn't afford to send her boy off to one of the coasts and pay for the tuition — if Frank would even be allowed in.

Anna proved her resilience again, though. She found Frank a part-time job working for a civil engineering professor named Allan D. Conover at the University of Wisconsin. It wasn't architecture, but it was the next best thing. Conover taught Frank the basics of engineering and allowed him to work on real-life problems. He also convinced Frank to enroll as a special (aka unofficial) student in the civil engineering classes, which he did. For a little while.

From Disaster to Chicago

Remember how, as Frank watched and admired the construction of the Wisconsin state capitol, the dome caved in, crushing and killing almost everyone inside?[1]

That happened during this time—his stint at the University—and it marked the moment that Frank got his first glimpse at tragedy. (Sadly, tragedy would haunt Frank like a loyal but unwanted dog throughout his life.)

The sight, which haunted him in his dreams, affected both his human sympathies and his architectural goals.[2]

You may recall why the tragic incident occurred: The building contractor had tried to cut corners by putting inferior materials inside the dome's main supporting columns.

Frank was disgusted. It was then that he vowed to make every one of his buildings with quality and integrity, so that they would be safe and strong for years and years to come.

However, Frank didn't stick around college for long in his quest to become a great, quality architect. He stayed only for about a year, claiming the classes were boring and weren't giving him any real-life experience. He was ready for the big times, for the "real world."

He told his mother he wanted to go to Chicago, the city of architectural innovation in 1886, and asked her to contact his Uncle Jenkin who was having a new church built there for his ministry. Anna didn't want to, worried she would lose her boy forever if he went so far away, but he convinced her it was the only way to fulfill their mutual dream. Uncle Jenkin essentially said "No way!" in his letters,[3] predicting (perhaps aptly) that Frank would waste his time on women and clothes. Frank was insulted, and it made him all the more determined. He hocked some of his father's books and his mother's prized mink collar (sewn into his coat by Anna herself to satisfy her son's odd fashion sense), bought a train ticket with most of the money, and struck out for Chicago with only seven dollars to his name.[4]

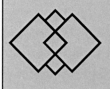

Fast Fact: A dollar went a lot farther back when Frank first arrived in Chicago in 1887. One of Frank's dollars was worth somewhere between three and four of today's dollars, and things were a lot cheaper. Still, it wasn't much money to live on.

Frank took the train from Madison, Wisconsin, to Chicago, Illinois, with his head full of visions of the grand buildings he would create, the interesting people he would meet, and the high life he would live as the star architect his mother dreamed he would become.

So, why did Frank want to go to Chicago in the first place? Well, something big was happening in the architectural world at that time. Something very big — skyscrapers.

Architects like William Le Baron Jenney, Daniel Burnham, and Louis Sullivan were constructing buildings around steel frames. Steel served as a stronger support system than wood or brick, so buildings constructed around steel could go higher — much higher — than ever before. A new style was emerging called the Chicago School. The architects behind the Chicago School wanted to show off their cool new steel frames, so they didn't add much to them, keeping the buildings the same simplistic, skyward-reaching shape of the frames themselves and just adding lots of large, plain windows for decoration.

Many famous buildings came from this movement, but the one Frank was perhaps most interested in was the recently completed Home Insurance Company office building erected by famous architect William Le Baron Jenney in 1885; it was the tallest office building in the world at the time.

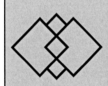 **Fast Fact:** The Home Insurance Building was the very first building in history to be framed completely out of iron and steel.

The revolutionary Chicago School sprang from the ashes of the 1871 Chicago fire that had nearly destroyed the whole city. People were still rebuilding and expanding when Frank arrived 15 years later, and architects were in high demand.

Jenney, his friends, and his contemporaries fascinated Frank. He wanted to work for them. He wanted to be their rising star, just as he was in his mother's eyes. It didn't turn out that way right off, though. Frank, a Wisconsin farm boy at heart, got a major culture shock when he stepped off that steam engine.

The city was dirty and dark, without a trace of his beloved nature in sight. He wiped the ugly vision from his eyes and replaced it with his fantasies. He was going to be a great architect, and this was the place to do it. But Frank got a little caught up in the fast pace of the city.

First, he went to the ballet, which cost him one of his precious dollars. Then, he took a tour of the city in a cable car. Then, he had himself a fine meal before checking into a hotel for the night. When he woke to set out on his job search, he realized he had only three dollars left. Frank didn't let it get him down. He would be fine, right? He'd get a job no problem.

He bought himself a bushel of bananas,[5] telling himself it was all he would eat until he found a job, and then he began walking the street looking for just that.

Silsbee and Corwin

It wasn't as easy as he expected. Yes, there were architect offices all over the city, but they all turned him down. There weren't any open positions, and Frank had no past work history or a college degree — not to mention that on the first day, he forgot to bring his sample drawings with him. Some people told him they'd be interested in talking to him again in a week or so, but Frank didn't have a week. His taste buds had grown rather weary of bananas.

On the fourth day of searching, Frank walked into J. L. Silsbee's office. Silsbee was the architect designing the All Souls Church, ministered by none other than Frank's uncle, Jenkin Lloyd Jones. Frank knew this, and according to him, he had avoided Silsbee's office until he absolutely had to. He didn't want to get a job just because he had an "in" with one of Silsbee's big clients. So, even though it most definitely would have helped him get the job, Frank didn't mention the connection. It didn't matter; Silsbee hired Frank as a "tracer" or draftsman. He saw something in him; perhaps he picked up on the raw talent or the single-minded determination behind Frank's eyes.

Frank was delighted, of course, but he couldn't celebrate just yet. Pay day wasn't for a week, and his banana bushel was growing thin. Another young architect in Silsbee's office noticed the worry and hunger on Frank's face one day not long after. His name was Cecil Corwin, and he made a friend of Frank that day by buying him corned beef hash at a restaurant — a meal Frank would crave and savor for the rest of his life. Corwin then went above and beyond common courtesy by inviting Frank to stay in his guest room and even lending him 10 dollars to put inside a letter sent home to his mother.[6]

The two young men connected over music, literature, architecture, and their backgrounds. Both were minister's sons. They both wanted to be great. So, instead of studying books on architecture, they roamed the Chicago streets to observe great craftsmanship firsthand. They both fell in love with the work of Louis Sullivan.

Sullivan was a man after Frank's own heart, and it showed in his simplistic, yet grand buildings. Sullivan, too, had grown up on his grandparent's farm and had fallen in love with the shapes of nature. He was the partner at a firm that created large, beautiful public buildings. At that time, he was working on the new Auditorium, which was an office building, a fancy hotel, and an auditorium all rolled into one. Sullivan's designs were simplistic shapes, like the ones Frank played with in the Froebel gifts. His only ornate decoration was the elaborately sculpted archways he created at the top of his buildings. The Celtic-style carvings on those archways evoked images of the flowers and other plants that Frank remembered from his time on the farm.

Honesty Is the Best Policy

After working for Silsbee for less than a year, Frank had received two raises[7] (one obtained after actually leaving Silsbee's employ for a short time) and could now afford to move his mother and littlest sister Maginel to Chicago. Jane was already living independently as a school teacher. Around this time, he also took up his first ever construction project, the Hillside Home School, for two of his aunts.

Despite his success at Silsbee's office, Frank grew discouraged. He respected Silsbee, but he didn't think Silsbee was crafting the best buildings that he could. He always drew out beautiful, elegant designs for each client's building that awed Frank with their genius, but the buildings never ended up looking like the drawings. The client always seemed to want something more simplistic, traditional, and plain than the pretty pictures, and Silsbee let the clients dictate how the building ended up. In fact, to Frank, it seemed that Silsbee didn't really care about the creation of the building at all. He drew up the pictures for his own pleasure and then handed them off to other people, requesting that they stick to the plan if it was possible, but not really caring if it didn't end up that way.

While this sounds like normal business practice, it didn't sit well with Frank. He didn't believe in the "the customer's always right" mentality. He didn't believe in just drawing up pretty pictures and not making sure they came to fruition. He thought a man ought to create the best thing he possibly could, and if the clients were allowed to dictate the design or if corners were cut during the execution in the name of what came easily, how could he ever hope to achieve his very best?

Frank shared his complaints with Cecil Corwin, but Cecil didn't get it. He told Frank architects have to be practical if they want to make any money. They had to do what the client requested if they wanted the client to come back. Frank found the whole process dishonest and discouraging. It went against the Lloyd Jones' family's motto: truth against the world.

Then, Frank found out that Adler & Sullivan, the office where Frank's and Cecil's idol Louis Sullivan worked, was hiring. Frank felt guilty about leaving Silsbee after he had given him his first job, taught him much, and taken good care of him, but he told himself it was necessary. If he wanted to be an innovator, he had to align himself with other innovators, and Silsbee was old school. Silsbee didn't think out of the box like Sullivan did. Silsbee's work was safe and ordinary.

So, Frank applied for the draftsman job at Adler & Sullivan, and he didn't go about it half-heartedly either. He marched into the office and demanded to speak directly with Sullivan and Sullivan only. This was not the policy. Sullivan never talked to new draftsmen; he was far too busy. But Frank had the tenacity of a bulldog. He wouldn't give in. Eventually, Sullivan came out to look at Frank's drawings himself, the ones he had crafted while working for Silsbee. Sullivan didn't like any of them, but he did like Frank and his enthusiastic, persistent personality. He told Frank to come back in a week with new drawings. Frank worked night and day, and it paid off. Sullivan hired him.

Sullivan became a mentor to Frank. Frank called him *Liebermeister*, which is German for "beloved teacher." The two were nearly inseparable, bonding almost immediately over their fervent love of architecture and pushing its boundaries. Sullivan, who rarely talked to anyone, would talk to Frank about designs and plans until well after hours. Sullivan taught Frank about William Morris' theory that the shapes found in nature were the key to creating new, wholesome architecture — something that really hit home with Frank the farm boy. Sullivan himself believed in "organic whole" architecture, meaning that the parts of a building ought to come together seamlessly and naturally, like musical notes coming together to make a beautiful harmony.

Sullivan's partner, Dankmar Adler, was the engineer who brought Sullivan's artistic dreaming to life. Though Frank didn't bond with Adler in the same way he did Sullivan, Adler built upon the teachings Frank had learned in Professor Conover's office and taught Frank how to actually make his wild imaginings a reality.

Frank took all of this teaching to heart and applied it to his newfound goal: to create true American architecture. Frank had noticed that most of the buildings being crafted around him were essentially knock offs of European architecture, like those cathedrals his mother framed above his crib. Frank wanted to create something new, something wholly American, and Sullivan was one of the few people who was doing just that. Frank wanted more than anything to join him. Frank's enthusiasm didn't go unnoticed, and Sullivan allowed Frank to take the office right next to his.[8]

Sullivan handed over a lot of responsibility to Frank. Sullivan preferred to work on large, grand, public buildings like the Auditorium. So, he handed over the domestic clientele to Frank, allowing him to build homes for wealthy clients, even though he was hired on as a draftsman, drawing up designs. Between 1890 and 1892, Frank designed and oversaw the building of about half a dozen houses for Sullivan's clients, getting paid overtime. The extra money was a welcome site to Frank, but it would vanish almost immediately, spent on luxuries like books and Japanese art.[9]

Sullivan also allowed Frank to work alongside him on the Auditorium building. Frank got to draw out all of the ideas that Sullivan dreamed up but didn't have the time to draft himself. Sullivan also asked Frank to help him work on the Transportation Building to be displayed in the 1893 Chicago World's Fair.

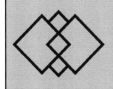

Fast Fact: **Sullivan's favoritism of Frank ended up getting him bullied. When Frank began to stand up for himself, it lead to a vicious brawl where Frank emerged the victor but was stabbed in the neck with a drafting knife in the process![10]**

Frank had found his paradise. He was an architect, a real architect, working under a teacher who shared his ideals. He had found a mentor who allowed him and even encouraged him to break boundaries, utilize the full power of his imagination, and create honest architecture exactly the way he wanted to.

Sources

1   Wright, 1977.

2   Wright, 1977.

3   Huxtable, 2004.

4   Thorne-Thomsen, 2014.

5   Thorne-Thomsen, 2014.

6   Huxtable, 2004.

7   Huxtable, 2004.

8   Thorne-Thomsen, 2014.

9   Huxtable, 2004.

10   Huxtable, 2004.

CHAPTER 4
HOME AND FAMILY

Lovestruck

Frank had been rather sheltered by his mother, and hers was the only female attention he had any experience with. In fact, when he'd first gone off to college, it wasn't the work or being away from home that scared him. No, it was the idea that he might have to talk to girls. An independent, reclusive boy since childhood, he had never had a large number of friends, and he wasn't very social anyways. He wasn't much good at striking up conversation with anyone, let alone a pretty girl.

That's why when Frank and Cecil went to a costume party at Frank's uncle's All Souls Church, Frank never expected to bump into his future wife. Quite literally. Dressed as a French army officer to go along with the *Les Misérables* theme, in high-heeled black boots, tight white pants, a sword, and a gold embroidered red coat and cap, Frank rushed across the room to say hi to some friends after a bit of dancing. A beautiful girl with gold-flecked red hair and wearing a pink peasant's dress rushed across the dance floor at the same time, looking behind her at a friend. She and Frank bonked heads right in the middle of the dance floor. Frank accidentally struck the poor girl so hard that she fell down.[1]

Dizzy and embarrassed, Frank helped her up and tried to apologize, but she insisted it was her fault as much as his. Her name was Catherine Tobin, Kitty for short. She introduced him to her parents, who invited him for dinner the next day. He arrived with a lump on his head, and found himself treated with genuine courtesy in her house. He also observed that Catherine was the darling of the family, and got just about whatever she wanted — a lot like Frank himself, except her parents actually had the money to give her things. Despite her privilege, she didn't come across as spoiled, and Frank found that charming.

After dinner, she asked Frank to go out with her to look at the buildings in a fashionable new neighborhood. As they strolled the streets together that night, looking at architecture, Frank was smitten. It wasn't long before he asked for her hand in marriage. But neither his family nor hers approved. They were far too young, Frank only in his early twenties and Kitty in her late teens. While they *were* young, there were probably ulterior motives in play. Anna didn't want to lose her precious boy after only just moving to Chicago to be closer to him. Catherine's family didn't want their darling girl to marry a poor architect who was terrible with money.[2]

In an attempt to get Kitty to forget Frank, they sent her off to live with a relative for three months. However, Frank and Kitty only saw this as a romantic obstacle that their love could easily overcome. Both Frank and Kitty were used to getting what they wanted and sweet-talking their parents. The separation only made them more insistent on getting married.

Their determination paid off. Both families relented, seeing no other option, and the two were married on June 1, 1889, the same year Sullivan completed his grand Auditorium with Frank's help. Catherine wasn't quite 18, and Frank was a week shy of his 22nd birthday. Many people wept during the ceremony, and not all of the tears were happy ones.[3]

Newly married, they needed a place to live. Frank's good friend and mentor, Louis Sullivan, provided the answer. Frank had told him that the wages he was earning wouldn't support his new bride or buy a house. There was no way Sullivan was going to lose his gifted prodigy, so he gave Frank a new five-year contract at work and a loan to build a house.

Frank picked a lot in Oak Park. The neighborhood's prairie scenery reminded Anna of home, and according to Frank, "That settled it." He found a corner lot that already had a small cottage on it for Anna to live in. Then, he built the house for himself, his wife, and their future children. Frank spent more on the construction than was in the budget — something that became a bad habit for him that angered many of his clients.

During construction, Frank and Kitty had to stay with Anna in the Chicago home Frank had procured for her. Anna was a regular monster-in-law, though after how she treated William, that really wasn't a surprise. Kitty was taking her boy from her — even though she would be living closer than the nearest next door neighbor. Anna put the already pregnant Kitty down for everything she did. When she heard Anna coming, Kitty took to hiding in closets.[4] Luckily, she got along very well with Frank's youngest sister, Maginel, who was still living with her mother. Still, it must have been a great relief to Kitty when the house was complete and they could move in, away from Anna's constantly judging eye.

Oak Park, Illinois

Oak Park was a fairly new but rapidly growing neighborhood populated by the affluent, white collar class: bankers, stockbrokers, executives, and manufacturers. Essentially, they were the people in charge. Some of them were commissioning skyscrapers for their offices, essentially sponsoring the radical architecture change — new American architecture. It is unsurprising that many of these folks became Frank's future clients. However, when Frank first moved in, their domestic taste needed some updating.

The houses of Frank's neighbors in Oak Park made him turn up his nose. The high fashion of the time was Victorian style homes with elaborate, over-the-top exteriors. Such houses were made out of a hodgepodge of materials: bricks, wood, plaster, ironwork, stone, and shingles. The result was, in Frank's opinion, a massive eyesore full of porches, balconies, chimneys, and castle-like towers that took away from the natural beauty of the prairie lands they stood on. Frank called them gingerbread houses, and there was no way his house would look anything like them.

He'd made many houses for Sullivan's clients at this point, but now, he would get to craft whatever his imagination could dish out for his own home. Unsurprisingly, he drew from those long-ago Froebel gifts. The front of his house was dominated by a large but simple triangle raised on a rectangular base. He combined Sullivan's teachings of organic architecture with the Shingle style he'd learned at Silsbee's office. He chose rich brown materials (brown bricks and cedar shingles) to blend his house with nature. To give his house an elongated look to match the vast, wide prairie around him, he added a long band of windows across the front of the triangular piece that would allow him to see out onto the plains.

Frank wanted the musical harmony of Sullivan's organic architecture to carry to the interior of the home, too. He kept things simple — no pretty but useless knickknacks and figurines for him, no boxy rooms packed to bursting with furniture. He kept the color scheme simple and natural: golds and greens. His open floorplan (something craved by homebuyers today but unheard of at the time) made his six room house seem much bigger. His rooms flowed seamlessly together, creating a wide open, prairie-like space. When he could, he made the furniture part of the house, making his bookshelf, his table, and his cabinets jump out of the wall. These "built ins" are another thing modern people actively seek out and request, and the idea sprang from Frank's own head. He used flowers and plants for decoration rather than flashy chandeliers and giant furniture.

Frank made his fireplace the centerpiece — literally. It was exactly in the center of the house, and he made a little nook for family gatherings around it, called an inglenook, which was separated from the rest of the house by curtains. Above the fireplace, he carved words to live by: "Truth is life," and under that, "Good friend, around these hearthstones speak no evil word of any creature."[5]

An inglenook is when there is a space on either side of a fireplace, making the area look more roomy and cozy.

Children and Creativity

Frank also created a drafting room for himself upstairs with the bedrooms so he could draw and create plans as he pleased from the comfort of his home. It was a luxury he had to give up quicker than expected, as he and Kitty had six children (Lloyd, John, Catherine, David, Frances, and Robert Llewellyn) one after the other. There were so many children in the house, and Frank and Kitty were still so young that the disapproving neighbors often commented that it was a house full of children with no adult supervision. Some also whispered about the odd house behind their hands, but others marveled at the fresh design and asked Frank if he might design a house for them.

Frank had to turn his drafting room into two tiny bedrooms to accommodate his babies. That wasn't the only adjustment he made for his children, either. He was always adding onto the house as new ideas came to him… even when he didn't actually have the money. In the year of the World's Fair, 1893, he created the Playroom, set off from the house by a dark, narrow hallway that led into the grand 20-foot-high, open space dancing with light from the band of windows encircling it. The wood floor was patterned with squares and circles. There was a massive fireplace with a mural of the famous book *Arabian Nights* above it. Glass globes hanging from the ceiling caught the light and shimmered. It was a fairytale room filled with toys that left a lasting impression of fond memories in his children's minds.

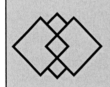 **Fast Fact: Frank's eldest child, Lloyd, also grew up to be an architect, and in his memoir, he recalls that some of his happiest childhood memories happened in that Playroom.**[6]

Frank, who had grown up poor in a simple home, wanted to surround his children with beauty and luxury. He decorated his house with Japanese paintings, Chinese vases and bronze statues, and Indian carpets. These imported goods didn't come for cheap, but Frank, who had never had money, didn't know how to manage it. He was always adding to and decorating the house with the money the family needed for groceries. He was making $60 a week under the new contract with Sullivan, which was unheard of for a draftsman, yet Frank racked up debt almost as fast as he had children. Instead of paying the bills, he would buy an Indian statue or a Japanese screen, proclaiming that he couldn't live without them.

This spending became a compulsion, and that compulsion urged him to borrow from others. One day, he had depleted his funds so low that he couldn't afford a train ticket home to Oak Park from Chicago, where he worked. So, he went to his cousin Richard, who worked in the city as well, and borrowed the money for a ticket. A few hours later, he showed back up on Richard's door with some new Japanese artwork in tow, asking for more money to actually buy a train ticket this time.[7]

Frank needed some extra money, despite how well Sullivan was paying him. He also wanted to explore his own creativity and take on projects that were entirely his own. Frank had found that he loved working on houses, but Sullivan liked to focus on public buildings. Frank started to take on extra clients behind Sullivan's back — something expressly forbidden in that generous five-year contract Frank signed.

These houses served as a transition period for Frank. They were an odd mixture of his own radical ideas mixed with popular trends requested by his clients. Later, he would refuse to bow to client requests and would tell them that if they wanted him they'd have to let him create exactly what was in his head, but on these early houses, he couldn't afford to tell clients no. Still, in all of them, he enforced an open floorplan rather than boxy, closed-in rooms, and he simplified the requested styles as much as possible.

Projects as big as houses can't go unnoticed for long, though, and Sullivan found out about Frank's side jobs. He was furious. He felt betrayed by one of his dearest friends and his most trusted artistic confidant. In his anger, he refused to hand over the deed to Frank's Oak Park house. Sullivan lent him the money for it, remember? He had held the deed as collateral, and now he refused to hand it over even though Frank had managed to pay off the loan by this time.

He might never have relinquished it, had Adler (Sullivan's engineer partner) not calmed him down and persuaded him. Though Sullivan saw the unfairness of holding the deed, he didn't forgive Frank for what he'd done, and Frank was rather angry at him now, too. Sadly, Frank's actions tore a terrible rift between the once close friends, and they didn't speak for nearly 17 years.[8]

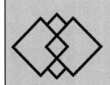

Fast Fact: Tragically, Sullivan's final years were spent in poverty and depression. His Transportation Building was not well received at the 1893 Chicago World's Fair, as his American architecture was a radical concept that didn't match with the Renaissance-style work displayed there. This and Frank's betrayal pushed him into a deep depression that caused his business to decline rapidly.

Frank left Adler & Sullivan in 1893 and got his own Chicago office in the Schiller building, sharing it with his good friend Cecil Corwin. Frank wasn't in the office all that much, though. He just used it as a meeting place. He preferred to work at home, surrounded by the inspiration of his own piece of paradise and his family.

Left entirely to his own devices, not having to answer to anyone, Frank blossomed. He could take on the clients he wanted and let his imagination run wild. He began producing bizarre, never-before-seen work that would shape the course of architecture as we know it, and made sure everyone in the architectural community knew the name of Frank Lloyd Wright.

This is a house Frank built in Oak Park.

Sources

1 Wright, 1977.

2 Huxtable, 2004.

3 Thorne-Thomsen, 2014.

4 Huxtable, 2004.

5 Thorne-Thomsen, 2014.

6 Huxtable, 2004.

7 Huxtable, 2004.

8 Huxtable, 2004.

Chapter 5
The Designs That
Shaped the World

Organic Architecture

Striking out on his own was a risky move. Frank had to procure new clients fast. His big break came in the form of William Winslow, a businessman and amateur architect. He found Frank's work fascinating and let him do what he pleased — a dream come true for Frank.

The house he created was a marvel. He stuck to his beloved organic architecture, making the house long and using horizontal bricking around the unusual tile siding to mimic the long lines of the surrounding prairies. Long windows kept the house looking sleek. The feature that drew the most attention to the house was the roof, which appeared to float on top like a hovercraft.

The house delighted Winslow and many others who saw it. People began to speak Frank's name with wonder, and it appeared his budding business was safe.

When he designed his own studio at Oak Park, Frank took organic architecture to a whole new level unthought-of by Sullivan. As Frank's business grew, he needed more space. Remember: He had given up his private drafting room as his number of children grew from three to six.

So, in 1898, he created an addition for the house and made it a private studio. It was a thing of bizarre beauty, with an octagonal library and a floating balcony held up with a chain and weight system engineered by Frank.

The problem arose when Frank went to build the passageway connecting the studio to the house. A huge, beautiful willow tree stood right in the way, and Frank couldn't bear to cut down such a magnificent natural artifact. So, Frank turned his problem into an unusual masterpiece. He built the passageway around the willow. Its branches poked up out of the ceiling. Talk about organic architecture! The whispering on Frank's street started all over again,[1] curious talk about the odd man who had a tree inside his house.

However, Frank's odd architectural choices in his own house and others made him even more popular among his neighbors with a wilder imagination, and by the time he was 30, Frank was a popular, talked-about man in the neighborhood with a growing reputation as a rising star architect. Everyone, whether they loved it or found it bizarre, wanted to hear about his organic architecture ideals. His talents and his unusual architecture spread by word of mouth, and more and more people wanted to know what it might be like to live in a Frank Lloyd Wright house. Frank's popularity skyrocketed.

All the talk garnered him the attention of a Chicago architectural big-shot named Daniel Burnham. Burnham told Frank that he wanted him in his firm and that he would pay for Frank to go study European architecture firsthand in Europe for six years with his whole family in tow. After he completed the years of study, he would come back and have a guaranteed job with Burnham.

It was a huge opportunity. A man who could shell out that kind of money could give Frank the steady flow of income he needed to support his large family. He would be guaranteed work — something that he lacked while working for himself. This job meant security for his family … but Frank couldn't take it.

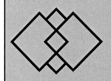 **Fast Fact:** Burnham was the lead mind behind the White City of the 1893 Chicago World's Fair in which Sullivan's Transportation Building just didn't fit in.

He didn't want to mimic European architecture. Though he and Sullivan had parted ways, Frank still believed in Sullivan's vision of creating American architecture. Burnham only worked in the classical European style, and Frank decided he would rather continue the somewhat uncertain path he was on and allow his imagination to craft new and exciting things than compromise his art and his beliefs for a steady paycheck.[2]

Prairie Houses

Frank kept on creating houses like his own and the one he'd created for William Winslow: long, subtly simple houses that blended with the nature around them. A ladies' magazine first wrote about what Frank called his "prairie houses" in an article about a house he'd designed for a famous publisher, Edward Bok, and they became his calling card. Frank sold a lot of designs to Bok, which Bok put in his magazines, spreading Frank's fame much farther than Chicago.

For these prairie houses, Frank built in horizontal lines and always inserted bands of windows to mimic the wide plains. He often made some of those windows pale-colored stained glass depicting natural landscapes and patterns. He never painted over his building materials, keeping the wood and clay brick natural to blend with the earth and the trees. The outside always had patios and terraces that Frank turned into mini-gardens full of flowerbeds and other plants in order to blend the house into the surrounding nature.

He never included an attic or a basement. Those places were for cramming unwanted items that ought to be thrown away, and his homes were no place for throwaway items. Remember: Frank liked clean, open spaces free of the European-style knickknacks and fancy furniture. His houses sprang straight from the earth with no basement in between, and his roofs jutted over the edges of the houses, reaching for the prairie earth and giving off that floating effect that everyone admired on the Winslow home.

Inside, he held religiously to his open floor plans. The main living areas, like the dining room, living room, and study, all connected to each other in a wide open space separated only by the fireplaces he always put in the center. Sometimes, he created walls that didn't quite touch the ceiling, to give off an effect similar to the Japanese screens he loved so much.

As the popularity of these houses grew, however, their connection to nature often became metaphorical rather than literal. People in the suburbs and cities with no prairies in sight asked Frank to build prairie houses for them. There, the houses didn't actually blend with surrounding nature, but they mimicked the look of nature, and that was good enough for Frank.

Nothing like these prairie houses had ever been seen before. Frank was always reading, learning about new architectural trends, and stowing away the best bits and pieces in his imagination and his heart. He not only absorbed the best of what the other odd, eccentric architects like himself were doing, but he also memorized what was good about styles that the more traditional architects used. For instance, he never forgot the beautiful, natural wood of those shingle-style houses he built for Silsbee.

Of course, no matter how good an architect he became or how far and wide his popularity grew, Frank was never completely satisfied with a design when it was finished. He always wanted to improve or change something about it. His clients were plenty satisfied and didn't want to dish out any more money for Frank's improvements, but Frank's perpetual dissatisfaction and perfectionism can be seen in how many times he remodeled his own Oak Park home.

Frank's mind was a marvel in that he didn't just cram all these bits and pieces of other people's work that he liked into one crazy, jumbled design. He didn't copy. Instead, he absorbed the ideas, mulled them over, tinkered with them, and brought them back out into his own work in an entirely new way. All of the knowledge he accumulated sprang from his imagination newborn in a style crafted deep within his own heart, mind, and memories.

But if anyone asked Frank where his ideas came from, he would say they'd sprung entirely from his own imagination.[3] In his mind, the great Frank Lloyd Wright didn't need any outside help or influence. The truth is far more beautiful and impressive, but Frank never outgrew the desire to prove his mother right — that he was special, an architect from birth who needed nothing and no one but his own resolve and talent to pull himself up out of poverty to greatness and acclaim.

As a result of this unadmitted imitation and adaption, Frank's prairie houses grew to incorporate arches, a feature always present in Sullivan's architecture. In 1902, Frank's neighbors, the Heurtleys, asked him to make them a house that would cause people's heads to turn in the streets.[4] So, Frank turned heads by making the front door off-center and wrapping it in a grand archway. He also made the huge fireplace in the center of the home an arch, so that the flames in the grate looked like the heart of a captured sun. Frank also created a new bricking technique for the home, where he alternated two kinds of bricks to make it look like the house was wrapped in brick ribbons. Even more radical of a design choice was placing the living room and dining room upstairs where the bedrooms always went. Always sure to add an organic touch, Frank made part of the ceiling lighted glass so that one could look up and see the sky even inside the house.

Next, Frank's neighbors, the Cheneys, approached Frank about designing their house. Edwin and Martha (everyone called her Mamah) were Frank's dream clients. They didn't care if their house didn't blend in with the others on the street, and they let Frank try out whatever design ideas were swimming around in his head. So, Frank made their house contrast completely with the Victorian homes surrounding it. He made it long and low, with a long brick wall shielding the lower half of it from the road. The backyard sloped downward so Frank created a second story that looked like a single story from the road. The Cheneys loved the deceptively spacious home, and Frank struck up a friendship with Mamah Cheney as a result.

Frank began to build prairie houses for people all over the country. However, one of his most famous was built in his current home state of Illinois. The Avery Coonley House had a playroom much like the one Frank had built for his own children. This playroom was surrounded by stained glass windows designed with all of the shapes in the Froebel toys to make an eye-catching pattern. As a special surprise for the Coonley children, Frank hid a little American flag in one of the rectangles for them to find later.[5]

Frank began to get serious recognition in the architectural community during the turn of the century. He became a member of the Chicago Arts and Crafts Society, and his designs appeared so prominently in the Chicago Architectural Club's exhibitions in 1894, 1895, and especially in 1898 that many other architects complained that Frank was getting more showtime than he deserved. In 1906 and again in 1908, he was featured in the Art Institute of Chicago.[6]

As early as 1901, Frank began to give lectures on his ideals for the new American architecture. He encouraged other architects to take advantage of the new advancements in building materials like steel and reinforced concrete. He spoke out about the need for a new style of architecture that suited the American needs and represented America itself. Since his work was heavily featured in respected magazines, people began to listen and observe his style. According to Frank, there should be no attic or basement in a home. Windows should be the out-swinging style that opens naturally and easily out into nature rather than the encased guillotine style that opens up and down.[7] Ceilings and doorways should be brought down to human scale rather than rising taller than any man who's ever lived.

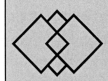

Fast Fact: Frank used his own height as a measuring tape for how high to make his ceilings and doorways. He was five-foot-seven, so he raised that slightly to five feet eight and a half inches and used that distance as the basis for his ceiling height. This became a source of frequent complaint from his taller clients, but Frank simply ignored them.[8] It was more natural this way, more organic.

Despite his growing prominence in respected exhibitions and magazines, Frank outright refused to ever enter his designs in a competition. He believed that such contests were judged by a committee of average people to please the average audience, and thus the best and worst were never even considered in favor of the average.[9] Frank, considering his work (justifiably) above average, saw no point in being a part of such mediocrity.

From the Prairie to the City

By 1903, Frank had grown his business so much that he employed a loyal staff of seven. He'd actually had far more employees than that in total, but most of them came and went very quickly. Employment under the much-talked-about Frank Lloyd Wright and working on his steadily growing number of commissions was enough to make any young draftsman, tracer, or architect salivate. However, Frank was not the best at paying his employees. One of his employees admitted that they all just had to "hang on by the teeth," pinching pennies until Frank remembered that he actually had to pay them.[10] So why did they stick around? Well, Frank had inherited the same charm that his father, William, had used to hang on to his jobs and his family for as long as he did. Frank, though, had the added advantage of being expressly talented and increasingly prominent. Many of his employees were in awe of him, and his charm kept employees and clients alike coming back for more despite his eccentricities.

His mother and his wife, however, were not as willing to let his discrepancies with money slide. When things got particularly bad, Anna would pester him about his foolish money decisions. She didn't want to see her boy bedraggled and destitute like his father had been when he'd been unceremoniously shoved out of her doorstep. However, Anna wasn't the best disciplinarian when it came to Frank. All he had to do was essentially wait her out; she couldn't stay mad at her golden boy for very long.

It was tougher to smooth things over with Kitty, and she played sneaky and dirty. Fed up with Frank coming home carrying beautiful things they didn't need while they struggled to pay off the debts left by Frank's many add-ons and adjustments to the house, she sent their daughter Catherine into Frank's studio while he was trying to impress a very upscale client. Catherine, who had been playing outside, and was covered in dirt, popped her chewing gum in her mouth, held out her hand, and said, "Mama needs a dime." Frank didn't have a dime. Not a single dime. Catherine, coached by her mother, was insistent and kept asking for the dime while Frank squirmed in front of the fancy client. At last, Kitty came to fetch little Catherine, but she'd made her point.[11] Sadly, it didn't do much good. Frank never had to learn to change his ways. He was a master at charming his way out of ugly situations. He could get creditors to leave his house laughing. He could get cops sent by contractors and clients to collect on debts to wait just one more day.

So, with his little group of talented employees and his rising fame in the world of domestic architecture, Frank simply began to expand his horizons to the public sector instead of reforming his ways. Now, Frank would always love building homes most of all, but when the Larkin Company of Buffalo, New York approached him to work on a new office building for them in 1904, he didn't refuse. Mr. Larkin was a very open-minded person, and he was willing to let Frank do whatever he thought was necessary.

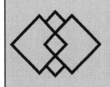

Fast Fact: **The Larkin Company was a mail-order soap outfit, a revolutionary idea for the times. Of course, just delivering soaps to people's doors doesn't sound much like big mail-order companies of today like Amazon, but the Larkin Company was one of the pioneers of this style of shopping well before the days of the Internet.**

Frank saw the Larkin Administration Building as a temporary house for the employees, whom he saw as "one great official family,"[12] and he was determined for it to be both comfortable and safe. Frank was still plagued by the horrendous scene of the dome collapse at the University of Wisconsin, and he went above and beyond the ordinary call of an architect's duty to make this office building safe and sound. He did his job so well that he created the first entirely fireproof office building built entirely of brick and stone and furnished with metal furniture.[13] By making the whole space air-tight, he also made it one of the first completely air-conditioned buildings in all of America and protected the employees from the smog coming off the trains nearby.[14]

He didn't entirely abandon his prairie style, though. He made the first floor a wide open space for all of the secretaries to work in together, and he made sure the place was well lit and connected to the outside world with a giant skylight. The managers worked in private offices on the upper floors, and balconies jutting out over the main office space allowed them to observe their staff easily. He tried to make life simple for the employees, and he even went so far as to design trash cans and telephones specifically for the building. Unfortunately, the company had already ordered those types of items in bulk.[15]

Much later in life, Frank would create a housing revolution with his care for the ordinary person. He'd already created office buildings for the working class, so why not combine that with his passion for domestic architecture and create homes for the working class? Frank's unusual and beautiful take on an affordable home became known as the Usonian style, more commonly known as the American ranch style. His first clients were Herbert and Katherine Jacobs of Wisconsin. He took their working class budget and made exceptional use of every penny.

For a cheap heating system, he ran water pipes underneath the floors in a technique called radiant heating. He put the source of all the electrical wires, plumbing, and gas in one place. In usual Frank style, there was no basement or attic. He even made the roof as minimal as possible, simply squeezing insulation (which usually goes in an attic) between roofing material, but still made sure to create that floating effect from the long ago Winslow House by using his signature banded windows. Instead of an expensive garage, he created an elegant carport. The sky lights, wrap-around windows, and central fireplace kept the nature-oriented prairie style alive in a house created for half the price. The house was so beautiful and the style so popular that the Jacobs family actually started charging people admission to see the house.[16]

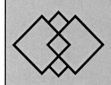 *Fast Fact:* **Frank based his second Usonian home off the hexagonal shape of honeycomb cells to keep the house in tune with nature. Even the tables and beds were created in the six-sided shape.**

However, about 30 years before that, back in the early 1900s, Frank's public urban buildings, crafted with concern for the everyday man, were not nearly as well received. When it came to establishing a new modern architectural style, the rest of the world was faster on the draw than America. The Larkin Building received a staggering amount of press both in America and around the world, but many Americans didn't understand it. Russell Sturgis, a very popular architecture critic at the time, called it ugly. Many Americans shared his sentiment, but leading architects in the modernist movement from around the world, such as British architect C.R. Ashbee and Netherlands architect Hendrik Berlage actually travelled overseas to see it in person.[17]

This is a bay window in a house that Frank designed and built in Oak Park.

Still underappreciated by the very people whom he was trying to benefit with his simplistic, organic work, Frank began to grow restless. From that restlessness would spring the first real scandal of many to come in Frank's unusual life.

Sources

1   Thorne-Thomsen, 2014.

2   Thorne-Thomsen, 2014.

3   Huxtable, 2004.

4   Thorne-Thomsen, 2014.

5   Thorne-Thomsen, 2014.

6   Huxtable, 2004.

7   Wright, 1977.

8   Huxtable, 2004.

9   Wright, 1977.

10   Secrest, 1998.

11   Secrest, 1998.

12   Wright, 1977.

13   Thorne-Thomsen, 2014.

14   Wright, 1977.

15   Wright, 1977.

16   Thorne-Thomsen, 2014.

17   Huxtable, 2004.

Chapter 6
A New Life

Leaving Oak Park

Things with Kitty were no longer idyllic and sweet. The redheaded girl in the pink dress was rubbing her head as though she'd been bumped in the middle of the dance floor all over again, and when she opened her eyes the finely dressed boy who'd once helped her to her feet was now withdrawing from her, leaving her alone on the floor.

Kitty started her own kindergarten, teaching Froebel's principles, to try and earn some extra money, but she held the classes in their home, and Frank constantly found children in his way. Frank, having grown up with an absent and withdrawn father, became a withdrawn father himself. He didn't like being called "Papa," which was what Kitty had taught their children to call him. He found the word grating. It made him feel old.[1] He lost himself in his work and didn't pay much attention to his many sons and daughters.

In his writings, he referred to his children as "her" children, meaning Kitty. He also seemed to think that Kitty had devoted herself so entirely to their children that she had lost love for him.[2] Sound familiar? It should. William made the same complaints about Anna in regards to Frank himself. However, Kitty wasn't prone to violent rages like Anna was; she was merely overwhelmed with trying to keep track of six children while her husband lost himself in his own head and designs. Still, Frank didn't feel loved by her anymore.

Those debts he was so slick at avoiding were beginning to catch up with him. Kitty was fed up with his spending, and the two began to fight more and more often. The kids took Kitty's side, just as Frank had taken Anna's.[3]

Frank's passion for his prairie houses began to wane just as he really started getting acclaim for them. Frank was always looking to improve, and he grew bored of crafting houses in the same style over and over again. He grew tired of his home life as well. In his autobiography, Frank talks of his growing unease and states that he still loved his kids and his home, but he tellingly makes no mention of still loving Kitty.[4]

Remember Mamah Cheney? She was Frank's neighbor and friend, and she and her husband, Edwin, had hired Frank to build their house in 1904. Well, in the years that followed, she became a bit more than just a friend.

Frank asked Kitty for a divorce, and she refused. She said that if he hadn't changed his mind in a year, she would agree. A year passed, Frank asked again, and Kitty still refused.[5]

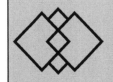

Fast Fact: **Kitty's refusal to divorce Frank probably came from practicality. Back then, women couldn't get the same kinds of jobs men could, and the jobs they could get didn't pay nearly as well. Kitty probably knew Frank would leave the child-rearing entirely to her, and she wisely worried about having to support six children all on her own.**

Frank's frustration and desire to get away grew to a fever pitch. Then, in 1909, when Frank was 42, a German publisher named Ernst Wasmuth[6] offered to pay for Frank to go to Germany and build a new design portfolio.[7] Frank's work was still not widely accepted by the American public, and Frank could now go study the widely popular European style that he and his mother had admired back in Wisconsin and come up with new ways to adapt that style into his own.

Frank probably saw architecture like that in this picture, which was taken in Dresden, Germany.

By this time, many younger architects were copying Frank's prairie style, and it didn't feel like his anymore. It was boring. He sank into what might be interpreted as a mid-life crisis. His enthusiasm and charisma began to slip, and he lost two major deals in the middle of the design process: one with the famous Henry Ford and the other with Harold F. McCormick, an heir of a prominent, high-class Chicago family.[8]

He saw Wasmuth's offer as his ticket out, and he jumped on it immediately. Frank up and left his wife and his children with very little warning. His justification for his abandonment was that a loveless marriage was worse than slavery and to protect such a thing was barbarous.[9] So, he left Kitty to deal with his huge pile of debt. He abandoned some of his clients in the middle of projects. He handed over his business to Hermann von Holst, whom he barely knew and who had no idea how to create in Frank's style. Thankfully, after Frank left, one of his employees, Marion Mahoney, saved a good number of the ongoing projects, and thus, Frank's business reputation … at least somewhat.

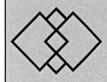

Fast Fact: In another eerie replication of his father, Frank left his family when his youngest child, Llewelyn, was just turning six. William left his family when his youngest child, Maginel, was six.[10] Perhaps Frank, somewhere deep inside, thought it was expected of him, or that he could not avoid it.

Maybe Kitty could have recovered from Frank's sudden abandonment, but Frank took an extra stab at her heart by taking Mamah Cheney with him when he left Oak Park in 1909. They'd been having an affair for a few years at that point, and hadn't exactly kept it hush-hush.[11] Still, the fact that he'd taken Mamah off to Europe with him when he'd said he was leaving to further his career and follow his passion had to hurt. He'd officially chosen Mamah over Kitty.

What did Martha (Mamah) Cheney look like? She was often described as beautiful and fair, though many of the pictures of her that eventually came out in the papers weren't very flattering.[12] Since she had soft brown hair, strong eyebrows, high cheekbones, a long, thin nose, and a sharp mouth,[13] one might even describe her as aristocratic-looking.

Mamah abandoned her husband and two children to follow after Frank, something the family-oriented Kitty would never have dreamed of doing. Kitty's world revolved around her children, while Mamah was more interested in art and intrigue.[14] She was an intelligent, trilingual college graduate with a passion for the arts — something else Kitty didn't share. She was also cunning and a bit conniving. The method of her abandonment was rather sneaky. She took her children on a trip to Colorado to see a friend. Then, she told her husband to come pick them up, not saying why, and then headed back to New York to leave for Germany with Frank, leaving her children confused and alone with her friend.[15]

Mamah struggled with her decision to leave her children behind. She was also plagued by the extreme prejudice against affairs and divorce. Although she had felt guilty that her passion was not based in the home, eventually she found solace in the teachings of a Swedish feminist writer, Ellen Keys.[16] In today's world, she probably would have become a successful businesswoman, an art curator, or a famous writer rather than a stay-at-home mother. She had married her husband Edwin at the age of 30, after refusing his proposal twice before, simply because she was afraid of becoming a spinster. Roped into a life she had never really wanted, she was a bit ahead of her times.

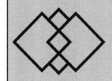 *Fast Fact:* **Mamah actually became great friends with her idol, Ellen Keys, and even helped her translate her work into English.**[17]

Mamah was a fiercely independent woman, and though she loved Frank and called him her soulmate, she didn't spend all that much time with him in Germany. After a few weeks there, she got a job as a language teacher at a German college while Frank moved on to Florence, Italy, to work on his design portfolio and only visited her occasionally. Frank eventually called his son Lloyd, then 19, overseas to help him as a draftsman.[18]

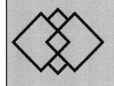 *Fast Fact:* **Lloyd left Frank's (sort of) alma mater, the University of Wisconsin, to come help his father, and by that time he was already very talented at drafting.**[19]

In 1910, Frank had pretty much finished his work, so he and Mamah moved into a villa together and enjoyed long, idyllic nature walks and quiet evening dinners free of scampering children and nagging creditors.[20] They traveled and admired sculpture, art, and architecture around Europe, all while Frank's pockets grew lighter and lighter, as usual.

Returning Home

Unbeknownst to Frank, a media storm of epic proportions was brewing back in Chicago. Word had gotten out in Oak Park that the famous Frank Lloyd Wright had abandoned his lovely wife and all their babies to go to Europe, and had taken his married mistress with him. These days, *TMZ* would have a heyday with that information for a week or so, and then it would be old news. Back in the early 1900s, that was unspeakable. It was social suicide. It was the scandal to beat all scandals.

The news spread much farther than the quaint little town of Oak Park, and soon every media man in Chicago wanted every juicy tidbit of the story. Poor Kitty was hounded day and night by the press. Despite the heartbreak of having her husband run off with another woman, Kitty stood by her man. She made public statements to the press with her minister beside her as support, saying that she had complete faith that Frank would return home. She said that Frank was merely off battling the "vampire" that had risen up inside him, but her Frank would beat it in the end.[21] She assured the media hounds there would be no divorce. She didn't believe in it, and she was determined to be there for her husband when he saw the error of his ways and came home.

The public was not as forgiving as Kitty, and Frank returned to Chicago in 1910 with a ruined reputation. Mamah's husband, Edwin, had had enough, too. He took full custody of the children and divorced her.[22] By moving back in with Kitty, Frank tried to act like he was a contrite family man who'd seen the error of his ways. However, he began to find it harder and harder to get new clients. In private, Frank also made it quite clear to Kitty that things were over between them. Frank's real plan was to run off with Mamah somewhere that the press couldn't keep sniffing around.

Frank's beloved mommy rushed in to save him again. She purchased land on the top of Frank's favorite hill in the Helena Valley, where Frank had grown up working on the Lloyd Jones' farm.[23] Frank borrowed some money from Darwin Martin, a loyal client who worked for the Larkin Company, and set to building a new house for himself and Mamah. Anna, unsurprisingly, made plans to leave her little house near her grandchildren to be near her boy again. Frank didn't want to leave Kitty and their kids without an extra source of income, though, so he converted the studio into a living area so that they could rent out the main house for extra money.

The Taliesin Home

Frank began construction on the new home right away, trying to keep it under wraps. However, a journalist got wind of it in 1911 and wrote an article about the love nest. The rumors started flying. Frank's spoiled reputation nearly cost his aunts, Nell and Jane, the Hillside School that he had built for them. When people found out the family connection, they began to withdraw their children.[24]

Still undaunted, Frank didn't give up construction. This new house was to be his masterpiece. Following the Lloyd Jones' traditions, he even gave it a name: Taliesin, after the Welsh druid priest who was renowned for singing poems about the fine arts.[25] The druid religion centered on nature and the elements, so Frank designed his hillside house to contain the elements of earth, wind, water, and fire. The walls sprung straight from the earth, practically carved into the hillside. He took his open floor plans to new heights so that air would flow freely through every room without hindrance. He installed multiple water fountains in the garden, and a stream ran through the back as well — if not the same one he used to float his shoes upon as a child, then very near it. Never one to forget a fireplace, Frank crafted numerous hearths in the grand stone fashion of the ancient Welsh to honor his family's history.[26] He did not want his house to be *on* a hill; he wanted it to be *of* the hill.[27] So Taliesin curved around the hill and popped out of it, just as the piano in his children's Oak Park playroom jumped out of hole in the wall.[28]

Frank may be thinking of Welsh hillside cottages like this one.

He planted orchards and fields and built barns and cottages for the workers he hired to tend them. Taliesin was his home, his workshop, and his personal piece of paradise.

The Marring of Taliesin

After some of the gossip died down and Mamah established herself as a perfectly good mannered, intelligent, and charming person in the Wisconsin community, people started to take notice of Frank in a positive way again. Taliesin was a marvel, and it reminded people of Frank's unduplicatable natural talent. He began to get commissions again, and by 1914 he'd landed himself a cushy and respectable gig designing the Midway Gardens in Chicago. The city had a large German population and the officials wanted to create an entertainment complex that would appeal to them by harkening back to German beer gardens.[29] Frank made the place an absolute dreamland. There was a winter and summer garden, restaurants, dance floors, a theater stage, and an area for concerts. Nature, sculpture, and elaborate craftsmanship collided to create an Eden in the middle of the city.

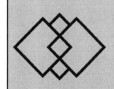 *Fast Fact:* **The Midway Gardens proved too expensive to keep running, but when the city tried to tear it down in 1929, they had a very hard time of it. Frank had done his job too well, and the complex did not come down easily.**[30]

It was while Frank was putting the finishing touches on this fairytale place that a horror movie played out in Taliesin. It was August 15, 1914.[31] Julian Carlton was a new handyman at Taliesin, recommended to Frank by the owner of Midway Gardens. Julian's wife Gertrude did the cooking, but it was Julian who served the food. It was said later that Mamah didn't like Julian for a reason she couldn't quite put her finger on.[32]

No one knows exactly what set Julian off — whether he was rebuked or if Mamah actually fired him and his wife — but on that day in August, he snapped. No one is certain the order in which the seven murders were carried out. There is some indication that he was mentally unstable; his wife recalled that he'd been acting very odd in the days leading up to the murders — sleeping with his hatchet in a bag by his bed and muttering about murder.[33] What is known is that he served lunch to the workingmen, Mamah, and her two children, John and Martha, who had come to visit for the summer. Then Julian whipped out a hatchet and killed Mamah with a single blow to the head. Her son was killed in his chair. Her daughter was killed while trying to run out of the screened patio for help. Julian set the whole porch on fire and moved on to the workers.[34] Seven men were inside the house eating lunch: the foreman, two draftsman, the gardener, the carpenter, and the carpenter's thirteen-year-old son.[35] The two who survived remembered seeing gas running under the door leading to the courtyard. Before they could react, it was set ablaze by an unseen hand. All the doors and windows had been locked. The men who were able crashed through the windows, but Julian was waiting for them on the other side with his hatchet.

The carpenter, William Weston, whose son had just been slaughtered, survived because Julian hit him with the blunt side of the hatchet. Despite their injuries, he and the gardener, David Lindholm, managed to run a mile to the nearest neighbor's house and get help. Lindholm later died of his burns. The other survivor was one of Frank's draftsmen, Herbert Fritz, but he was severely burned and had broken his arm jumping out of the window and was unable to help as Weston returned and held a hose on the blaze.[36]

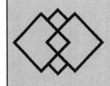

Fast Fact: Oddly, many accounts differ on how soon Carlton was caught and how soon afterward he died in prison, but all agree that the police found him inside the unlit furnace of the house. He'd swallowed acid, but it hadn't killed him. He died of starvation, refusing or unable to eat.[38]

Frank rode home on a train in shock. His son John was with him for support. Edwin Cheney, Mamah's ex-husband, had been notified of his children and ex-wife's deaths. He was on the train also. At first, all Frank knew was that there had been a fire, but there were journalists on the train, talking excitedly about the great mass murder story they were all going to cover.[37] A terrible way to find out.

Frank's world shattered. For all his faults and regardless of the scandalous way he and Mamah had come together, he truly loved her. The house he'd built just for her was a charred ruin — dead and buried with her. He plucked all of the flowers out of her garden and filled up her casket and the wagon carrying it with the bright blooms.[39] Frank told the few people in attendance that he wanted to fill in Mamah's grave by himself. So he worked into the night doing just that. He didn't make a gravestone because, as he put it, "Why mark the spot where desolation ended and began?"[40] To him, Mamah had been the symbol of newfound freedom, a new life. Now that new life and the masterpiece he'd created to represent it had been burned away to ash and buried beneath the fresh dirt atop an unmarked grave.

Sources

1   Wright, 1977.

2   Secrest, 1998.

3   Huxtable, 2004.

4   Wright, 1977.

5   Wright, 1977.

6   Huxtable, 2004.

7   Thorne-Thomsen, 2014.

8   Huxtable, 2004.

9   Wright, 1977.

10   Secrest, 1998.

11   Huxtable, 2004.

12   Huxtable, 2004.

13   Thorne-Thomsen, 2014.

14   Huxtable, 2004.

15   Huxtable, 2004.

16   Huxtable, 2004.

17   Thorne-Thomsen, 2014.

18   Huxtable, 2004.

19   Huxtable, 2004.

20   Wright, 1977.

21   Huxtable, 2004.

22   Thorne-Thomsen, 2014.

23   Huxtable, 2004.

24   Secrest, 1998.

25   Wright, 1977.

26   Thorne-Thomsen, 2014.

27   Wright, 1977.

28   Thorne-Thomsen, 2014.

29   Huxtable, 2004.

30   Huxtable, 2004.

31   Huxtable, 2004.

32   Secrest, 1998.

33   Secrest, 1998.

34   Secrest, 1998.

35   Huxtable, 2004.

36   Huxtable, 2004.

37   Huxtable, 2004.

38   Secrest, 1998.

39   Wright, 1977.

40   Wright, 1977.

Chapter 7
Ups and Downs of
Love and Life

A New Muse ... or Mistake

Frank received many letters in the aftermath of the tragic murders, but he only responded to one. It was written by a woman named Maud Miriam Noel, and Frank at once picked up on an "artistic-intelligence" in her words.[1] He arranged to meet her, and his intrigue only deepened. Miriam, as she preferred to be called, was a divorcée, and she talked to Frank about her failed marriage. She was mysterious and sophisticated, able to match his wit and talk about deep subjects. From a rich Southern plantation family in Memphis, Tennessee, she had a love for the finer things in life, just like Frank. She liked to sculpt, and she believed strongly in the spirit world, often consulting with mediums,[2] making her by far the most interesting (if the most odd) woman Frank had ever encountered.

What did Miriam Noel look like? She had reddish brown hair, an average round face, and her greenish eyes were close together, but it was her fashion sense that set her apart and turned heads — not unlike Frank. She liked turbans and scarves, draped herself in shawls and beads, and wore furs over long gowns. Add the monocle and the ever-present cigarette, and Miriam strikes a very unusual image indeed.[3]

Frank was intrigued, and he and Miriam started the next in his string of affairs. Kitty still refused to divorce him. After the tragedy at Taliesin, she had softened toward him and allowed their younger children to go see him. She even offered to keep house for him, but he turned her down.

The affair with Miriam started in the same year of Mamah's death. Frank was lonely and forlorn, and he believed he'd found a kindred spirit. However, Miriam was a morphine addict, and her mental state was even more unstable than his own mother's had been. She, too, was prone to fits of high passion and anger. She could tell that Frank was not over Mamah, and it bothered her. Frequently threatening to break off the relationship, she would send Frank nasty letters detailing just how horrible he was.

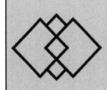

Fast Fact: **Back in the early 1900s, morphine was used as a common painkiller like Motrin® or Advil®. No one was aware of how highly addictive and dangerous it could be. It can also lead to depression.**[4]

A disgruntled housekeeper leaked some of these letters to the press. Frank's reputation was in shambles again. He was even arrested under the Mann Act, which essentially meant he was arrested for committing adultery across state lines.[5] He got the rather silly charges dismissed, but he couldn't as easily dismiss the public's opinion of him.

Still, he didn't blame Miriam for any of this, and she went with him wherever he went for work, even all the way to Japan.

Japan and the Imperial Hotel

Japan had long been a source of inspiration for Frank. He'd always loved Japanese artwork, and he'd taken his first trip there in 1905. On a trip in 1911, he'd met a fellow art collector, Frederick W. Gookin, and the two bonded over their shared interests. It was he who'd recommended Frank when the manager of the Imperial Hotel began looking for an architect to build a new one. Frank had gone back with Mamah in 1913 to discuss the matter, but the plans were delayed until 1916. They came at a time when Frank was desperate for a large, well-paying project. He went back and forth to Japan over the years, planning the construction and making drawings, and then he finally got down to the heart of the business in 1918.[6] This time, Miriam came with him, along with his son John.

Construction wasn't easy. Frank could only speak to his clients and half of his workers through interpreters, and he soon had to rework his whole design because his clients wanted everything built in the traditional Japanese manner — done by hand. The working men had to use bamboo scaffolding as they built up the heavy bricks and concrete foundations.

Japan is known for earthquakes caused by Mt. Fuji. Once again, the image of that collapsing dome came back to Frank. He knew he needed to make this hotel a fortress that would be safe from the rage of Mother Nature. He made the base of the building wider than the top to keep it stable. He made floating foundations that would move together with the earth when it began to shake, rather than crumbling to pieces.[7] He added gardens and pools in the central, social part of the building where guests could gather. They were not only beautiful, but practical. The water elements of the design were meant to protect against a fire. He kept the rooms long and low like his prairie houses before and his ranch houses to come. This made it sturdier and closer to the ground, helping prevent collapse in a quake. Lastly, he made an odd but stunning roof out of pyramids laid with overlapping layers of greenish copper. He chose the copper over tile because he knew that when earthquakes hit, they often dislodged the heavy tiles and sent them flying through the air, destroying everything in their path.[8]

The hotel had its fair share of mishaps, one of which proved to Frank that Miriam was a psychic. She had been longing to go to a garden party held at the American Embassy, but when the day came, she felt strange and didn't want to leave the hotel. It caught fire that day, and because Miriam had stayed, she and Frank were able to save their valuables, including $40,000 worth of Japanese prints.[9] Thanks to Frank's safety measures, the fire was contained without too much damage, but Frank became all the more fascinated by Miriam after that.

He didn't complete construction until 1922, but his hard work paid off in a huge way. On September 1, 1923, the great Kanto earthquake rocked Japan. Tragically, 100,000 people died, and countless buildings throughout Tokyo crashed to the ground. Frank received a telegram from the Japanese government official who had backed the hotel, which said, "hotel stands undamaged as monument of your genius."[10] In fact, the hotel was in such good shape that it was used to house the homeless during the aftermath. Frank had fulfilled the vow he'd made at the University. He'd made sure his building was safe and strong. He saved lives through his art.

The Divorce Cycle

During their time in Japan, Miriam had given up sculpting and had thrown herself wholeheartedly into helping Frank with his work. There are even rumors that she made some of the textiles that he included in the hotel. Despite her mood swings and eccentricities, Frank was utterly devoted to her as well.

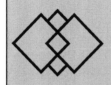

Fast Fact: Miriam's eccentricities are evident from a story told by one of Frank's friends, who witnessed Miriam lock herself away in her room during lunch after Frank made a joke about her needing to change her dress. She emerged hours later in a white silk gown and told Frank that from now on he needed a special costume to wear at dinner if he wanted her to eat with him. Frank took the request as a challenge, and he and Miriam spent all night designing a special white linen suit for him.[11]

Frank came back from Japan, his work complete, in July 1922. It was shortly thereafter that Kitty at last gave up hope that he would ever return to her. Now he had a second mistress who was whiling away the time with him over in Japan. So, she finally agreed to a divorce.

The Chicago Frank returned to, though, was unrecognizable. It was no longer a center for innovation. The rebuilding and expanding was pretty much done, and the architectural community had taken up the tastes of the more conservative architects who drew on the old European styles. Frank's work in Japan was hardly noticed in the U.S., though it garnered attention abroad. Frank had no more contacts. Everyone was either mad at him, scandalized by his actions, or had simply moved on; he'd been gone four years, after all. The public was no longer clambering for him to design their homes.

With the lack of work and financial strain, Miriam grew more restless than usual. Frank himself felt restless in the freshly rebuilt Taliesin. Even with new walls, it harbored ugly, painful memories. Frank's mother, who was living at Taliesin also, unsurprisingly made the already tense and unbalanced relationship with Miriam even worse. Anna, though prone to fits and overly passionate behavior herself, didn't approve of Miriam and thought she was changing Frank.[12] Like Kitty before her, Miriam felt that resentment, and it did nothing to improve her stormy moods. So, Frank moved to California and experimented with the new textile block and concrete styles. Miriam, of course, tagged along.

Anna died in February 1923.[13] The loss of his guiding light and the woman who'd been by his side the longest must have come as a crushing blow, despite the fact that he himself was 56 and she had lived a long life with her boy at her side. Despite the scandal surrounding Frank at the time, one can guess that Anna died happy. Her golden boy, her predestined little architect, had risen to greatness and acclaim just as she'd always dreamed he would. He'd made a name for himself, even if his personal life had tarnished it somewhat.

Frank spared no time in marrying Miriam. In fact, he only waited the time period required by law for remarriage after a divorce, setting the wedding for November 1923. Frank, a perpetual romantic, said "I do" to his bride at midnight on a bridge straddling the Wisconsin River on his property at Taliesin.[14]

Sadly, though, Miriam's physical and mental health began to decline steadily following the ceremony. Her own fits and moods became wilder. She was insanely jealous, always accusing Frank of being attracted to other women, and saw fit to punish him more and more both physically and verbally.

Despite her mood swings and the many times she ran away from him, Frank sought to win her back over and over. He believed that he had harmed her by drawing her into the scandal of being with a married man, and he tried his best to make up for the pain that he perceived he'd caused her. Frank sought the advice of a psychiatrist on how to help Miriam. Today, the psychiatrist might have diagnosed Miriam as schizophrenic, but instead, he told Frank he ought to free her for her own good. Essentially, he said that the way to save her from self-destruction was to leave her and free her of the strain their affair had put on her.

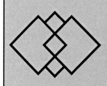

Fast Fact: In one of her episodes, Miriam got it into her head that Frank was falling for her Russian friend, Madam Krynska, and one night when they were all having dinner, she threatened the other woman with a gun that Frank had to wrestle out of her hands.[15]

If Frank intended to leave Miriam on the advice of the psychiatrist, he didn't get the chance. Miriam packed up her things and left just a few months after the marriage. But, like Kitty, she didn't actually divorce him. Perhaps her dramatic storming out of the house had been for show. Perhaps she had wanted Frank to come charging after her like a white knight. If so, the plan backfired horribly.

The Civic Opera House in Chicago.

Not long after, Frank ran into Olgivanna Lazovich Hinzenberg at a ballet at the Chicago Opera House. She was a dancer who had come to America from Paris to sort out some legal matters with her estranged Russian husband. She was exotic and charming, not to mention very young — only 26, while Frank himself was now 57. She had a daughter named Svetlana, and she was practical and sweet, rather than wild and passionate like Miriam.

What did Olgivanna Lazovich Hinzenberg look like? Her face was rather square but her cheekbones were prominent. She had dark eyes and long dark hair that she pulled back in simple fashions. Unlike the eccentric, fashion-forward Miriam, she dressed elegantly with a bit of ethnic flair, wearing embroidered scarves draped gently over her long locks.

The two moved in together after only a few months of knowing each other, and Olgivanna divorced her husband shortly after. Olgivanna's personality made for a much more soothing environment, and under her influence Frank started to thrive again. He took on business buildings: building a skyscraper office, a country club, and the Automobile Objective and Planetarium where people could park and observe a nice view of the landscape.[16] But Frank was never without financial strain. Taliesin caught fire again, this time due to a faulty wire, and Frank had to take out a mortgage on all his assets just to pay for the reconstruction.

In July of 1925, just a few months after Olgivanna moved in, Frank filed for divorce from Miriam on the grounds of desertion. Miriam was fine with this at first, but then she found out that not only had a new woman moved in to take her place, but also the new woman was pregnant. She flew into a rage like none Frank had seen before. She tried to get Olgivanna deported, and to escape Miriam's wrath young Olgivanna had to leave the delivery room shortly after bringing baby Iovanna into the world in December, still weary and feeling sick.

Miriam sued them both: Frank for physical abuse (there is no evidence that Frank was the abuser in the relationship) and Olgivanna for "alienation of affection" (in which she demanded $100,000). The suits were dismissed, but the legal hoops were exhausting for all involved. Miriam even managed to somehow get a warrant for Frank's arrest (probably on a charge similar to the one brought against him when he first started seeing Miriam herself) and broke into Taliesin.[17] She broke everything in sight until Frank finally got her forcibly removed from the premises.

Frank and Olgivanna eventually fled Taliesin to escape Miriam, but that was when the papers got a hold of the story. Frank's name was mud once again, just when things had been looking up. To make things worse, Miriam got Olgivanna's ex-husband in on the scandal, sharing a lawyer with him. He claimed his daughter Svetlana had been abducted by Frank and his ex-wife. Frank had yet again crossed state lines with a woman who wasn't his wife, and he and Olgivanna were arrested under the Mann Act. Even the children were taken to jail. The charge was dropped again, but now there was just no going back. His debts were mounting, and work was scarce. He had to sell off his prized collection of Japanese prints to stay afloat, but it wasn't enough to keep the bank from kicking him out of Taliesin.

They were homeless for a long time, with Miriam chasing them down wherever they went. They went back and forth with the bank for about two years, getting let back in and kicked out of Taliesin a couple of times. Frank incorporated his business as Frank Lloyd Wright Inc. with backing from his loyal friend and client Darwin Martin, and got his divorce from Miriam finalized.[18] At last, Olgivanna and Frank married in August of 1928 and moved back home for good. Frank had lost four years' worth of work in the drama.

The Great Depression

Just as soon as things settled down in Frank's personal life, the economy imploded and all of America was scrambling for a handhold in the mud to keep from sliding into a dark abyss of poverty and homelessness. The stock market crash of 1929 sent the country spiraling into an era of poverty and ruin known as the Great Depression. Everyone felt the effects. No private clients were hiring architects to build their homes; they were too busy trying to keep the homes they already had. The government was still hiring, but the government didn't want a bizarre thinker like Frank Lloyd Wright designing their buildings.

Breadlines were a common sight during the Great Depression.

Frank did get asked to display his work in the Museum of Modern Art in New York because he was still very popular in other countries. His work was displayed alongside Swiss and German architects who shared his tastes.[19] Frank began presenting speeches again to get his name back on people's tongues. As always, he spoke about his beloved organic architecture. Still, a spot in a museum and some speaking gigs wouldn't pay his ever-mounting debt.

Olgivanna provided the solution. She encouraged Frank to open up an architectural school so he could teach young men about organic architecture. Frank took it on as his next challenge and called the school the Taliesin Fellowship. It would be held right in his very own home. In the first year, 23 students came. Frank's work was very popular internationally, so many of the students travelled from different countries to learn from him. So, like his father taught music before him, Frank began to teach architecture out of his home. But there wasn't enough room for 23 extra souls in the house, and Frank was still deep in debt for the last two times he'd rebuilt Taliesin. Frank's solution? He had the boys build the additions as part of their classes, cutting back on labor costs. Frank also had a farm and large house to tend, and farmhands, maids, and gardeners had to be paid. But his students were paying to be there — $1,100 a year, in fact.[20] For four hours per day, Frank required the boys to load hay, work the garden, clean the house, and cook and serve the meals.[21] Essentially, he had them doing what he'd done long ago on the Lloyd Jones farm, threefold. He told the boys that working together was a vital skill every architect must learn because he must be able to command a team of workers in order to bring his designs to life.

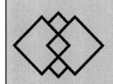 **Fast Fact: Frank made up a song called the "T-Square and Triangle Work Song," and the boys would sing it while they worked.[22]**

Frank didn't just use his students for free labor. He taught them a wide array of skills like pottery, sculpting, painting, textile making, woodworking, glassmaking, dance, drama, and music.[23] He taught them to work with their hands, whether it be the hard, sweaty work of loading up hay or the precise, delicate work of pottery. He taught them the value of hard work, he taught them the importance of fellowship, and of course he imparted his ideas about the necessity of organic architecture. At night, the boys with musical talent would perform concerts for the others. Frank also had guest lecturers and other performers come to entertain the boys.[24]

It was during this time that Frank began writing his memoir and reflecting on past work, deeds, and decisions. He started to think on the plight of urban families crammed together in large cities like Chicago. Frank was certain life would be more peaceful if everyone could just have his or her own slice of heaven: a piece of land to stretch out and grow on. He rallied his students, and together they created a model of a utopian city where all the inhabitants had their own pieces of land to grow their own food and connect with nature. Single people had nice apartments while families had homes big enough to accommodate every member. There was no big business in Frank's imaginary city — only local shops and businesses, with small private schools and little factories that couldn't over pollute the earth. Because everyone was surrounded by nature and no one was cramped in close quarters, Frank imagined his city would have no racism or crime or poverty. He called it Broadacre City, and when the model toured the United States in the '30s, it captured the hearts of the American people. There was talk of improving cities. New ideas came to life. And the eyes of America once again turned fondly upon Frank.

Sources

1   Wright, 1977.

2   Secrest, 1998.

3   Huxtable, 2004.

4   Secrest, 1998.

5   Huxtable, 2004.

6   Huxtable, 2004.

7   Huxtable, 2004.

8   Huxtable, 2004.

9   Secrest, 1998.

10   Huxtable, 2004.

11   Secrest, 1998.

12   Secrest, 1998.

13   Huxtable, 2004.

14   Huxtable, 2004.

15   Secrest, 1998.

16   Huxtable, 2004.

17   Huxtable, 2004.

18   Huxtable, 2004.

19   Thorne-Thomsen, 2014.

20   Huxtable, 2004.

21   Thorne-Thomsen, 2014.

22   Thorne-Thomsen, 2014.

23   Thorne-Thomsen, 2014.

24   Huxtable, 2004.

Chapter 8
Famous Structures

F rank's work, though not always appreciated in his own time, included many masterpieces that are still remembered, cherished, and mimicked today. His personal artistic highlights include the quintessential prairie house, awe-inspiring public gathering places, and futuristic pieces that are right at home in modern times, though they were dubbed bizarre upon creation. To truly comprehend Frank's talents, one must be familiar with the following famous structures.

Unity Temple

Right around the time Frank was finishing up the Larkin Building, he was commissioned for another public structure: a church for Oak Park's Unitarian community. The whole Lloyd Jones family was Unitarian, and thus Frank was more than happy to oblige.

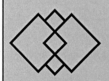 *Fast Fact:* Frank almost didn't get the Unity Temple job. The church committee at first wanted to hold a competition to select the architect (something Frank would never have participated in). Even after they dropped that idea, Frank would not have been the first choice if it weren't for the insistence of the committee head, mechanical engineer and inventor Charles E. Roberts, that they must have Frank.[1]

Starting work in 1905, it took three years to complete. Just like with the Larkin Building, he used this foray into the public realm to experiment with new design styles and building materials: cast reinforced concrete, a newly conceived material not yet used by many. Frank's insistence on working with this particular material caused many delays in construction because the expenses for such masonry exceeded the congregation's budget.[2] In Frank's mind, concrete was a good choice because it was cheap.[3] It was, but the tools and manpower needed to cast it into solid, massive shapes for building were not.

Another source of delay was Frank's shirking of typical church style altogether. He had to convince the pastor and committee to let go of the idea of a steeple. To Frank, a steeple served no purpose; it was just a symbol of man pointing to heaven. To convince the committee to forgo a steeple, Frank told them a parable of a man who climbed to the top of the tallest tree on top of the tallest mountain in an attempt to see God's face. As soon as he reached the tippy top, he heard the voice of God tell him to go back down, for the only place he could hope to see God's face was amongst his fellow people.[4] In telling this story, Frank convinced the committee that a symbolic reach for God is not necessary—God is among his congregation—so a church ought to be built for the functionality of the people of the congregation, and a steeple served no function. The committee's consensus was reluctant to say the least, but they let Frank do what he wanted.

For his design, Frank kept the imposing yet simplistic monolithic style of the Larkin Building, and crafted the church out of only a cube and a rectangle. The cube housed the auditorium for the services while the rectangle served as the parish house where the congregation could mingle and get together for church-held events. It seems utterly rudimentary at first, but nothing about Frank or his work was ever simple. The cube's top sloped slightly so that the highest point was in the center. Hidden inside the cube was a cross that ran up the aisles and branched off at the altar.[5] Several levels of seating arrangements created extra space for the congregation to move around comfortably.

Having a church service within concrete walls might not have created the right atmosphere, so Frank banded the inner walls with wood and his own built-in decorations. He brightened up the place with a skylight in the center of the cross and more windows at the tops of the walls above the arms of the cross, so that all light poured in from above like a divine beacon. The noise from the streetcars on nearby Lake Street concerned Frank, so he put the only entrance to the church in the back so that the worshippers would not be disturbed as they gathered at the door to greet each other and enter this holy place of solace.[6]

Frank thought that the services and the more casual events like Sunday school groups, church feasts, and other forms of entertainment needed their own space. He didn't want to spoil the simplicity of his noble cube auditorium to create more space for fun gatherings. So, the rectangular parish house or "Unity House," as he called it, was placed in the back lot and only connected to the auditorium by a shared entrance.[7] Inside the rectangular building, he installed moving screens that could be opened and closed to shut off sections of the room so that different Sunday school groups and events could take place at the same time and yet have their own designated space.[8]

With function always in mind, Frank made that shared lobby entrance lead the congregation to the sides of the auditorium, so that people showing up a little late would not disturb the rest of the enraptured audience. However, he added large exit doors next to the pulpit that were opened that the end of the service so that the congregation could pass and greet their pastor as they left rather than turning their backs on him.[9]

The Robie House

Though the name is spelled exactly the same, the Robie house was not built for little Robie Lamp, Frank's childhood crippled friend. Frederick C. Robie was a Chicago-based bicycle manufacturer who had very specific and unusual tastes in home design. Envisioning a playroom and walled garden for his children attached to a fireproof house that had a stunning, unobscured view of the city out the living room window, Mr. Robie couldn't really turn to anyone but Frank.[10]

He drove around Chicago and visited many other architects in their offices, but when he described his plans, they all scoffed and said the man he needed for an odd job like that was Frank Lloyd Wright.[11] The idea delighted Robie's wife, Lora, when he told her; she'd fallen in love with a prairie house Frank had built in her hometown.

Frank and Mr. Robie clicked over their shared interest in the new motorcars that were just beginning to become popular. The first time they met, they discussed Frank's own car, nicknamed Yellow Devil, and Frank was delighted with Robie's ideas for the house. This was also right around the time Frank's name was hauled through the mud after his affair with Mamah was revealed, so the work couldn't have been more welcome.

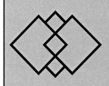 **Fast Fact: The odds of both men having a fondness for cars back in 1908 were very slim. Cars were a very new invention, and lots of people were terrified of trying to drive one.**[12]

The Robie's corner lot made Frank rework his typical style just a bit. It was long, narrow, and not all that big. It also backed right up into city streets on all sides. To create the space that Mr. Robie wanted, Frank had to make the house take up the entire lot. This meant the house had to be shaped like the lot. So, he made it long and rectangular, imagining it like a steamship floating through a sea of people traversing back and forth along the surrounding city streets.[13]

To protect the organic home from the raging urban sea outside, Frank surrounded the house with low walls that came to a point at either end of the rectangular structure, making the boat-shape even more prominent. There was a small garden inside the walls, with a set of stairs leading from the natural beauty of the earth all the way up to the second story of the interior beauty of the home. Mr. Robie's concern with safety rivaled Frank's own, so the home was made of brick and concrete to make it entirely fireproof. The bricks were formed out of prairie clay, and Frank didn't paint over them so that a flush of natural earthy color from the prairie could stand out in the middle of the city. He laid them horizontally in long strips and filled in the vertical space between them completely up with mortar the exact color of the bricks. Then, he cut the mortar between the horizontal sides very thick and very wide to mimic natural rock formations.[14]

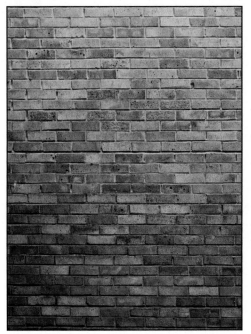

Never one to forget stained glass, Frank ran the windows around the length of the house and patterned them with a simplified geometric shape of leaves running along in a vine from window to window. He built planter boxes into the exterior walls and filled them with seasonal flowers; for if he couldn't bring the house to the actual prairie, he would bring the plants of the prairie to the house.

Staying true to his odd placement of front doors, Frank put the entrance to the home in the farthest corner from the street and hid it in a small, dark opening with a little walkway leading up to it. To someone who was used to seeing front-facing homes that displayed their welcoming and often ornate front doors to passerby, this cave-like entrance would probably look like a back door leading into a pantry or kitchen. To further confuse the everyday visitor, he placed a set of fancy gates on the side of the home that faced the driveway. However, if anyone tried to find the front door directly through these gates, she would find herself in a long, tedious passageway that eventually led all the way back around to that odd, hidden door.[15] Talk about privacy! Half the visitors might just give up and go on their way.

That dark, recessed front door worked its magic from the inside, though. Perhaps Frank liked those unsuspecting doors and the dark passages beyond them because they built suspense in all who entered. Then, when they immerged within the inner workings of his masterpieces, it looked all the more warm and inviting in comparison to that tiny black space. For the Robie House, Frank made it so that whoever entered the front door would see a bright light shining down from above a staircase that led into the heart of the home. In prairie-style form, the living space was a huge open area with a fireplace right in the middle, all lit naturally by the sun coming through the banded windows. At night, Mr. Robie could choose to turn on sunlights or moonlights installed side by side along the walls. The sunlights made it bright as day. The moonlights, hidden beneath patterned screens, gave off a subdued shimmering glow that mimicked the reflection of the moon on softly rippling water.[16] Because of the shape of the lot, nearly every room came to points on one or both ends, further creating the feeling that one was traversing a ship deck rather than a home.

As the final touch, Frank built his fellow motorcar enthusiast the largest garage in the world at the time. It could hold three cars at once; unheard of in a time when most people didn't even own one car. Frank never forgot the children of the home, and in addition to their own playroom, Frank made them a miniature garage just big enough for a toy motorcar, right next to their father's.[17]

The Robie House took two years to build, but when it was complete, it was hailed as the quintessential prairie house — a true masterpiece.

Hollyhock House

When Frank and Miriam ran off to California to escape the suffocating grief lingering in Taliesin and the hounding of the local press, Frank met Aline Barnsdall. She was an heiress of a wealthy family and had just purchased some gorgeous land on Olive Hill in Los Angeles. She had grand plans for the space, envisioning a children's play house, a theater, an apartment complex just for artists and actors, and a shopping center.[18] She thought Frank was just the man to do all those things for her, but first she wanted a beautiful house for herself and her family.

Aline was a wandering spirit who loved to travel. She had grand ideas, and she spouted all of them to Frank, but she was somewhat flighty and apt to change her mind in favor of the newest idea that had just popped into it.[19] Both started out very eager to work together on the home, but there were problems from the start. Frank had already been hired to design and build the Imperial Hotel in Tokyo, Japan. So, he was constantly traveling back and forth for four years. Aline herself loved to travel just for fun, so the two of them came up with the initial plans through a crazy game of telegram tag. While Frank was back in Hollywood, Aline was in Spain. While Aline was in New York or up in the Rockies, Frank was in Chicago or on a boat to Japan.[20]

The real problems arose when Aline, with the help of Frank's son Lloyd, hired a contractor that didn't understand Frank's designs. It didn't help that both Frank and Aline were constantly coming up with new ideas for the home and trying to incorporate them in the plans from halfway across the world from each other. The poor contractor didn't really know what to do, so Frank became angry with him. Aline was worried because the contractor was worried, and she badgered Frank with those concerns. Aline became angry with Frank because, ever since parting ways with Silsbee so many years ago, he didn't believe the customer was always right, and he rejected many of her ideas. He became annoyed with Aline in return because she kept changing her ideas and was listening to the contractor over him.[21]

However, the two creative minds of Aline and Frank at last came together to design something beautiful, and Frank even decided to take one of Aline's ideas to an eye-catching extreme. In one of her letters to him, she asked if he could incorporate her favorite flower, the hollyhock, into the design somehow. Frank, always eager to incorporate some form of nature into his work, put hollyhocks absolutely everywhere. He put real ones all over the many gardens surrounding the home. He studied the basic geometric shape of the flowers and simplified them into Froebelesque versions that he incorporated all over the house. He made concrete hollyhocks bloom out of the corners of the roof. He pressed the pattern into the plaster on the outside and into the concrete walls of the living room inside. He created special dining room chairs that had the flowers seemingly growing out of the backs. He had special carpets made with hollyhocks embroidered in them and hid the flower shapes in the stained glass windows of the home.[22] This abundance of hollyhocks is what gave the home its nickname.

He decided to make the house using concrete because it looked so much like stone, which would look natural on the flat western plains where foliage was scarce. The design was loosely based off of early American civilizations, with the addition of Frank's own personal flair, and he called it California Romanza.[23] A romanza is a short piece of instrumental music. Thus, within Hollyhock, Frank had combined the two biggest components that filled his childhood: nature and music. Hollyhock was a song created in honor the Californian desert landscape. He also painted the roof to match the surrounding desert landscape. Once again, Frank incorporated a very odd door, like he had for Heurtley's home back in Oak Park. Instead of making it off-center, though, he made it very low and made it open into a long dark hallway so that anyone who entered felt like he or she was exploring a cave. The hallway opened out into a large, bright living room that encapsulated Frank's beloved elements: earth, wind, water, and fire. The fire came from the grand fireplace — placed right in the center, as usual. The fireplace was made of concrete stones to pay homage to the land outside. To invoke the wind in the home, he built a skylight just above the fireplace. For the water, Frank built a pond inside the house. The little pond was shaped like a horseshoe and wrapped around the fireplace.[24] Though the living room was the main attraction, it was only one of many. The house included a music room, a library, special guest quarters, and a terrace on the roof.[25]

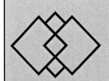

Fast Fact: Frank built four more houses while he was working in California, and he used concrete for all of them because he liked the way it looked on the desert plains. Those homes became known as the Textile Block houses. Frank actually invented a type of concrete construction for them that fortified hollow concrete blocks by weaving steel rods through the interiors, ensuring they would hold together securely.[26]

Aline had a daughter named Sugar Top, and Frank did his best to create a magical retreat befitting a little girl with a name like a sugar plum fairy. Everything in her bedroom, bathroom, and dressing room was child-sized just for her. She had her very own play porch off the dressing room so that she could play outside in the California sun and look out onto a child-sized garden she could call her own.[27] It was her personal little world tucked away inside her mother's massive, showy home.

Sadly, though, little Sugar Top didn't get to stay in her lovely new living space for long. Aline's traveling spirit won out, and she realized that it had been a mistake to create something so permanent for herself. Soon after the home was completed in 1921, Aline cancelled the plans for the theater, playhouse, and rentable living spaces in the middle of designing and construction, much to Frank's chagrin. Aline didn't just abandon the house, though; she gave it away as a gift to the city and asked that it be turned into a place for children to learn about the arts. Her wish was granted, and children still go to visit Hollyhock House and learn art within its walls.[28] Sadly, the state did not initially keep it up very well and allowed it to deteriorate before its true beauty was really understood or appreciated.[29] It was eventually restored and is, to this day, perhaps the most romantic home Frank ever created, so closely tied to nature that it burst from the very floor in a pond around the fireplace and bloomed from the walls in the simplified hollyhocks embedded in the plaster.

Fallingwater

One of Frank's most imaginative and futuristic pieces came about through a happy coincidence and what might be considered divine inspiration. It was built for the Kaufmann family, who had paid for the Broadacre City tour that put Frank back on the map. The Kaufmanns were the parents of one of Frank's students, Edgar Jr., and they invited him to visit them at their weekend home in Mill Run, Pennsylvania. Close by the family cabin, Bear Run Stream flowed downhill over rocky ledges that created gorgeous little waterfalls. It was one of the Kaufmanns' favorite spots on their land, and they brought Frank there. He was instantly captivated, brought back to the stream he played in as a child, building dams and floating shoe boats. He heard music in the waterfalls.

Kaufmann Sr. was a fan of Wright's work, and when Frank described the romantic home that was forming in his mind, Kaufmann Sr. was delighted and hired Frank on the spot. An ordinary architect would have built the house away from the steep, rocky stream bed and just allowed a grand window to look out onto it. Frank, being no ordinary architect, decided to build the house right on top of the stream, planting the house directly into the natural landscape he liked so much. There was a large rock ledge at the very top of this stream, and that's where Frank planted the house. He decided that it would reach out over the rushing waterfalls like the branches of any tree on the stream bank. He decided that a huge rock would serve as the center of the house and cement the home as part of the rock ledge it stood on, and the other rooms and elements would stem out from it like branches. He would build it entirely out of material found on the Kaufmann's land so that it would actually be a part of the landscape.

Frank Lloyd Wright 1867-1959 Fallingwater Mill Run PA

Architecture USA 20c

Fallingwater is one of Frank Lloyd Wright's most famous buildings
— it even made it onto a stamp!

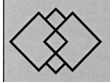 **Fast Fact:** A beam or plank that juts out over open space, held up only by support on one end is called a cantilever. Cantilevering is the technique Frank used to make Fallingwater look like it was floating over the waterfalls of Bear Run stream.

Frank kept the idea in his head but didn't actually draw it out until Kaufmann Sr. surprised him with a telephone call saying that he was on the way to see the drawings. Frank set to work immediately, but it was still not done when Kaufmann Sr. arrived. Frank's students took Frank's sketches and finished drawing up the actual plans while Frank distracted his new client with lunch and a tour of Taliesin.[30] Despite the last minute rush to put together concrete plans, the final product mirrored those feverishly sketched drawings almost exactly. The textured stone tower in the middle held up beige painted levels and balconies that stuck out like miraculously balanced Jenga blocks, adorned with Frank's customary plethora of windows to make sure the spectacular view could be seen from every angle.

Fallingwater, unlike some of his previous work, was instantly recognized as an artistic masterpiece even among the people of his own era. However, it was also the only building that Frank ever built that was not entirely safe. See, Frank's brain had outdone itself this time. This design he had imagined was so futuristic that the tools he needed to build it correctly hadn't been invented yet! The engineers had to basically guess how to bring the design to life, and they came up with methods that hadn't been tested. There should have been special steel frames to support the base of the windows underneath the cantilever that housed the bedroom. Concrete was still a fairly new thing back then, and Frank had only begun experimenting with it a few years previously. As a result, he and his workers didn't know how to properly reinforce it when it was poured into those unusual cantilever shapes.[31]

It's safe to say that Frank didn't realize that what he was making was unsafe. His mission had always been to provide homes for his clients that were not only beautiful, but also exceptionally secure — and he had always delivered. The simple fact was that according to the knowledge architects and engineers had back then, what he was doing made sense. There were some structural cracks that appeared during construction, but Frank simply made new calculations and patched them up. It's clear he had some idea of what he was doing, because even though he built Fallingwater without the proper tools, it held strong for nearly 60 years before partially collapsing.[32]

Taliesin West

In 1937, when Frank was getting on in years, his bones began to feel the unforgiving twinge of the freezing Wisconsin winters. The Fellowship was still going strong, and with the help of his young pupils, Frank had worked on a few minor projects in Arizona while he and Olgivanna had been banished from Taliesin.[33] Frank thought back on the warm Arizona weather, unmanageable in summertime, but very lovely in winter.

So, he bought some land outside of Phoenix on the flat top of a mesa in the middle of the desert. Frank designed a bold house with sharp angles and straight, hard lines, and his students built it from the ground up with their own hands. To keep the rooms from getting stuffy and miserable in the dry desert heat, the home and the school house were built out of canvas stretched between wooden supports rather than brick walls, so that the desert air blowing freely across the flat plains could cool the living spaces.[34] In the end, Taliesin West looked as though it was just another giant rock formation jutting out of the bare desert.

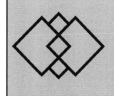 **Fast Fact: The building of this new home no doubt added a nice new pile of debt onto Frank, especially since his dear friend and past generous benefactor, Darwin Martin, had lost everything in the stock market crash that started the Great Depression.[35]**

It served as both a winter home and a schoolhouse, and Frank's students followed him back and forth from Taliesin to Taliesin West with the turn of the seasons.

The Guggenheim Museum

One of Frank's final projects was commissioned by Solomon R. Guggenheim of New York. His wealth had acquired him a substantial modern art collection, and he decided he wanted to display it to the world in a museum. Not just any museum would do; he wanted his very own, and he wanted it to be a true monument that encapsulated the spirit of the art within.[36] He also wanted it to reflect a new transcendental style of art called non-objective art. The idea behind the odd pieces was that the viewer would not be able to associate the shapes in the art with any known object, and it would thus break away the barrier between reality and transcendental harmony with the universe. To do this, there couldn't be any sort of distraction or barrier between the viewer and the art. Guggenheim asked Frank to craft a building that would connect the viewers to the art in this way.[37]

Frank was 76 years old when he took on the job, but in some ways his style was exactly the same as when he started — he still believed in looking to nature for inspiration. He decided to design the museum in the shape of a chambered nautilus shell, which is just a fancy word for the shell of the common garden snail. Frank wanted to capture the beautiful spiral shape within the museum, but he realized he would need to come up with a strategy to sell the idea to Guggenheim. The rich New Yorker wanted his museum to be a grand monument and temple for art, so Frank worried that he would reject shaping it to resemble an unassuming little snail. So, he told Guggenheim that he was going to build him a ziggurat. Ziggurats are ancient Mesopotamian temples, and they were built by creating a large base and then building a bunch of layers on top of it, each layer smaller than the last. Guggenheim got to think his museum was actually based off a temple design, when in reality, Frank flipped the ziggurat shape upside down to resemble a snail shell that starts with the smallest layer at the snail's back and branches out into a wide shell with a spiral design at the center.[38] Frank's design started out with a small base layer that widened and widened until it became a great glass dome with the spiral hidden inside the building.

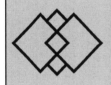

Fast Fact: Frank later quipped that he could hardly look a snail in the face anymore because he had stolen its home design right off its back for the Guggenheim Museum.[39]

With some clever white lies, Frank had convinced his client of the design's beauty, but he had a much harder time convincing New York City building officials. For one thing, it was hard to acquire a piece of land that would fit the huge design plan Frank had in mind, because New York was already so crowded. For another thing, nobody believed a design that was smaller on the bottom than at the top would actually stay up, and Frank's own engineers had to argue their case many times before anybody believed them. Frank also ran into trouble with his budget (as usual), which eventually led him to have to drop some of his design ideas for displaying the featured art pieces in the non-objective style.[40]

At last, Frank and his team received the right permissions, and construction began. When it was finished, the admiring public often took more notice of the museum itself than the art that it was built to house.[41] And there really is no wonder why. Upon entering the museum, visitors would be bathed in sunlight from a massive circular skylight that was separated into twelve pieces so that it mimicked the sun. The lobby floor was patterned with circles, like sunbeams dancing in the light cast from above. Recessed lightbulbs in the ceilings and walls were covered by triangular pieces of glass to incorporate another of Frank's favorite shapes from the Froebel gifts.[42]

Once in the lobby, visitors were led to an elevator that took them to the very top floor. From there, they would file down a spiraling ramp that lead them past all of the art in Guggenheim's collection. From the spiraling railings, they could look down and see the lobby floor or other patrons walking on the other side of the building as they traversed down each level. This created a sense of community between the art lovers. But he also created small spaces where only one or two people could stand very close to the art and observe it with care, creating a sense of privacy rare in such a crowded place as New York.[43]

The public loved the unique spiraling building, but the artists weren't nearly as delighted. The spiral shape made everything off-kilter. The only way to make a painting look like it was hanging straight was to hang it crooked, and the artists worried that this odd, shifting perspective would mess up the intended effects of their work.[44] The reason for this oddity, once again, was that Frank's mind was ahead of the times. He was using reinforced concrete again, and in the '40s and '50s, concrete was reinforced in imprecise wooden molds. To achieve this spiral shape in the way Frank imagined it and make the whole thing perfectly structurally accurate, he would have needed a computer drawing program.[45]

Frank spent the last 16 years of his life creating this beautiful and masterful building. Sadly though, he never got to receive the overwhelming praise of the public — so often absent in much of his work — because he died only six months before the museum officially opened for business on October 21, 1959.

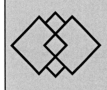

Fast Fact: Solomon R. Guggenheim actually died 10 years before the museum opened and seven years before construction even began, but the plans went ahead because he had made it a request in his will. His nephew, Harry Guggenheim, funded the project after his death.[46]

Sources

1   Wright, 1977.

2   Huxtable, 2004.

3   Wright, 1977.

4   Wright, 1977.

5   Huxtable, 2004.

6   Wright, 1977.

7   Wright, 1977.

8   Wright, 1977.

9   Wright, 1977.

10   Secrest, 1998.

11   Thorne-Thomsen, 2014.

12   Thorne-Thomsen, 2014.

13   Thorne-Thomsen, 2014.

14   Thorne-Thomsen, 2014.

15   Thorne-Thomsen, 2014.

16   Thorne-Thomsen, 2014.

17   Thorne-Thomsen, 2014.

18   Thorne-Thomsen, 2014.

19   Wright, 1977.

20   Wright, 1977.

21   Wright, 1977.

22   Thorne-Thomsen, 2014.

23   Huxtable, 2004.

24   Thorne-Thomsen, 2014.

25   Secrest, 1998.

26   Thorne-Thomsen, 2014.

27   Thorne-Thomsen, 2014.

28   Thorne-Thomsen, 2014.

29   Huxtable, 2004.

30   Thorne-Thomsen, 2014,

31   Huxtable, 2004.

32   Huxtable, 2004.

33   Wright, 1977.

34   Thorne-Thomsen, 2014.

35   Huxtable, 2004.

36   Thorne-Thomsen, 2014.

37   Huxtable, 2004.

38   Thorne-Thomsen, 2014.

39   Thorne-Thomsen, 2014.

40   Huxtable, 2004.

41   Thorne-Thomsen, 2014.

42   Thorne-Thomsen, 2014.

43   Thorne-Thomsen, 2014.

44   Thorne-Thomsen, 2014.

45   Huxtable, 2004.

46   Huxtable, 2004.

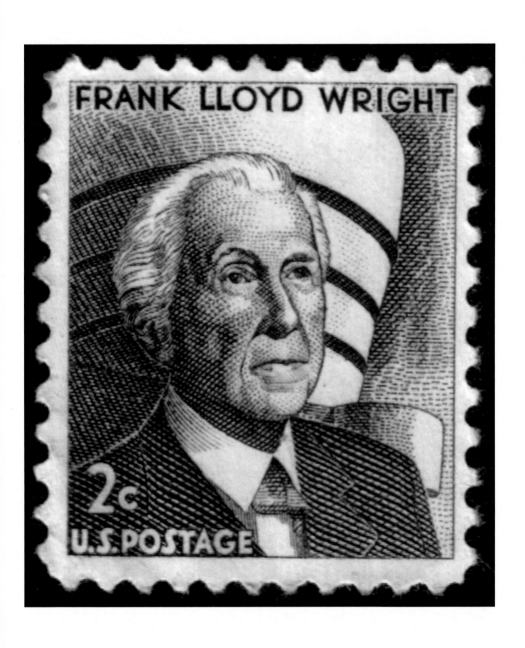

CHAPTER 9
AGING WITH STYLE

F rank didn't seem to know how to slow down, and he didn't seem to want to. Even as he achieved grandfather status and moved onward into great-grandfather territory, he remained relevant and prominent — whether with good press or bad. His energy is to be admired almost as much as his creativity. His later life saw much more acclaim than his early years, as the innovation and forward thinking that would lead to the Space Age began to catch up with Frank's own mind. Frank, though, never doubted his own genius, and thus he saw no reason to hold his tongue when it came to any matter of opinion. Sometimes, this paid off. Other times, it backed him into some seriously tight spaces.

Frank's Unpopular Revolution

Frank's rather large mouth got him into serious trouble once again in the early 1940s, right around the time he received the prestigious Gold Medal of the Royal Institute of British Architects (the American equivalent of which he wouldn't receive for eight more years) and a number of other recognitions from around the world as a result of his recent Usonian works.[1] World War II had broken out at the very end of 1939. Frank, tucked away at his two Taliesins and surrounded by his adoring pupils and loving wife, didn't give it much thought until America allied itself with Britain and joined the war after Japan bombed Pearl Harbor on December 7, 1941.

Frank did not approve in the slightest, and he made his thoughts known to his enraptured students, who absorbed the words of their respected instructor and spread them to the public. Frank's opposition to getting involved in the war that sought to overthrow Hitler might seem odd and wrong to many. However, there were a number of factors that contributed to Frank's views. The Lloyd Jones family had emigrated from Wales to America just two generations before because of British oppression. As a result, Frank didn't like the British very much — but he did like the Germans and the Japanese.[2] This had far less to do with their social practices and governments and much more to do with their architecture and art. As a young man, he'd grown to love the culture of Chicago, which was predominantly Germanic. The Midway Garden's project that he'd worked so tirelessly on had been created specifically for the German community. Frank's love of Japanese art and culture is also no secret. Japan was one of his biggest sources of inspiration, and his personal art collection overflowed with Japanese work.

The last straw was the draft, which required all young American men to join the army to fight against Hitler's forces. The boys of Taliesin's Fellowship were young able-bodied men of fighting age, and thus were required to put down their pottery, paintbrushes, and drafting pencils to pick up guns, grenades, and knives. Not only were those boys a main source of his livelihood, but also they were like his children — they ate, slept, worked, and played in his home. He didn't want to see them go, and he told them so. Many of them, emboldened by Frank's frequent impassioned, if somewhat irrational, speeches on the subject, declared themselves objectors of the draft and were thrown in jail.[3] It didn't take long for authorities to figure out that it was Frank who had inspired the boys to reject the authority of the government, and the local judge in charge of the Fellowship members' cases declared Taliesin West a commune for traitors and anti-Americanism. When accused, Frank couldn't resist preaching his beliefs, while at the same time denying the claims.[4]

This put Frank in serious trouble with the law under the Sedition Act of 1918, which punished people who interfered with war efforts or spoke disloyally against the government. One of the young men's parents blamed

Frank for their son's imprisonment and brought a case against him with the FBI, which led to J. Edgar Hoover declaring Frank a threat to national security. Hoover wanted to press sedition charges, but eventually was forced to give up when the federal assistant attorney general downright refused to prosecute Frank, twice.[5] Once again, Frank slipped away relatively unscathed. Old age hadn't taken away his charming touch.

Late Life Success

This last large scandal during World War II didn't affect Frank's business like the many scandals before it. As he got older, he became freer with his tongue, but it didn't always draw bad press. He was invited to speak at countless lectures at prestigious universities like Yale. His opinions on architecture became highly valued, despite the fact that terms like "crackpot" were also thrown in alongside praises of his genius when it came to describing him.

In 1957, he appeared on television, chatting with his old friend Carl Sandburg, a well-known poet in Chicago. Frank made quite a character of himself. He made it a point to argue against every subject Sandburg brought up, but he did it in an endearing and amusing way. When asked about the Washington Monument for instance, he called it "the act of an ignoramus … a point like a lead pencil."[6] But at the same time, he talked of valuing the artist and the emotions of the heart over the rigid logic of science — a romantic notion that rang of nostalgia for folks fast approaching the technological boom of the Space Age.

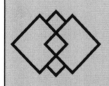

Fast Fact: Frank owed some of his retained popularity after the war scandal to the young female writer, Ayn Rand. She interviewed him many times over a number of years and published a book called The Fountainhead, and the main character (a heroic architect named Howard Roark), bore remarkable similarities to Frank. The best-selling book was so popular it became a hit movie.[7]

Due to his prominence in various types of press, work flooded in faster than Frank could complete it. Between 1949 and 1950 he had 600 commissions, and the offers didn't slow down. In fact, one-third of his life's work was completed in the last nine years of his life.[8] It seemed the public had finally come to appreciate him for the visionary he was.

He found new long-term clients in the Prices when he created the Price Company Tower for the oil and gas pipeline tycoon in 1956. The office building was Frank's own take on skyscrapers, which he had come to see as boring relics of the past.[9] He wanted to create one that was completely fresh, so he employed cantilevering once again. Every floor of the 20-story building cantilevered from the main skyward-reaching core at different angles and degrees, like branches from a tree. He ornamented it with green copper and gold-tinted glass. Frank turned 90 only one year later.

In his 90th year, he crafted his last well-known work: the Marin County Civic Center in San Rafael, California. Frank brought both beauty and function to this government building, setting it far apart from the boring, ugly concrete slabs occupied by many government departments today. Instead of leveling the two hills on the desired location, he built two wings that arched over the hills, connected by a round, domed room in the middle. Instead of stacking a bunch of vertical floors on top of each other to house the different departments, he made the office areas run horizontal to one another on only three floors, making sure each area had its own balcony space and a nice view. Frank mimicked a clear, sunlit sky using aquamarine ceilings trimmed with gold. Every story had glass walls that let in natural light and provided a view of the landscape. Roads ran through the ground levels of the arched wings, providing easy transport around the building, which had its fair share of courtyards with fountains and pools (Frank never forgot to add water somewhere).[10] The glass, colorful ceilings, arches, and skylights combined to create an explosion of color set to dancing by the playful antics of the sun.

Some critics and historians argue that Frank's later constructions lacked the same finesse, touch, and vision of his earlier work. In his prime, Frank had focused on beauty in simplicity, while near the end of his life, he splashed color and ornament all over his work (Aladdin statues, nautical shell museums, and rainbow fountains).[11] He crafted crazy, futuristic designs with a multitude of over-the-top elements seemingly just for the fun of it, rather than for practicality and function. Well, why on earth shouldn't a man approaching the end of his days have a little fun? Just because Frank's vision of the future wasn't sleek, silver, and streamlined like a rocket ship or a smartphone that nearly disappears when you turn it sideways doesn't meant it wouldn't have been an enjoyable one to live in. He was a romantic in an age of technological innovation, but instead of shunning the changes in American culture, he took up the futuristic visions, splashed them on his own canvas, and swirled them with romantic paint to create a color all his own.

The Love That Lasted

Frank's outspoken opposition to the draft also didn't stop apprentices flooding in from all over the world to join the Fellowship at both Taliesins. Just five short years later, in 1946, Frank had his largest group of pupils yet, totaling 65.[12] Frank selected them with the air of a secret society chairman. Young men and women interviewing to enter the Fellowship were usually turned away if they could not produce some sort of connection between themselves and someone else Frank knew. Even then, they had to be approved by Frank's appraising eye. If their hair was too short (Frank had always worn his own hair around his ears, much longer than the fashion) or if they went to a school he didn't like (Harvard, for instance), Frank might decide to turn them away.[13]

Fast Fact: One of Frank's many apprentices after WWII was an Italian prince named Giovanni del Drago. He didn't get any special treatment from Frank; he was made to work in the fields and the kitchens just like everyone else.[14]

But with so many commissions coming in and his body aging more and more each year, Frank didn't have the energy or the capability to run Taliesin on his own. Olgivanna Wright stepped up in a big way. In the early years of the Fellowship, she had served as a demure young wife who ran the household quietly from the background, but by the late '40s and on into the '50s, Olgivanna ran every aspect of the Fellowship. She set the rules for the apprentices, hosted grand events for Frank's growing number of important dinner guests, and made sure everything at both estates played out like a fine-tuned instrument.

It seems that she was just the woman Frank had always needed: equal parts intelligent, driven, and crazy. Like Kitty before her, she knew how to take care of her children and her household. Like Mamah, she knew how to take charge and summon everything she wanted right to her fingertips, and she was smart and cultured enough to match Frank's wit and share his interests. Like Miriam, she had a love of the arts and a hot temper. The right woman for Frank had to be a least a tad crazy to keep up with his eccentricities and get a handle on his chaotic lifestyle and terrible budgeting.

According to many Fellowship apprentices, she could be downright terrifying. Some called her manipulative and a control freak — some even accused her of trying to break up their marriages and verbally abusing people just to see how far she could push them. Others, though, simply called her strict but prone to over-the-top tempers, and even went so far as to call her a second mother. One apprentice, Bill Calvert, perhaps summed it up best when he said, "She wasn't an ogre. It's hard to convey. She was operating on a different principle. Her goals were to keep Wright going and Taliesin intact, and she did it brilliantly."[15]

She wasn't afraid to quell Frank with a look or some choice words, like when she scolded him in front of all his guests because he threw a temper tantrum about twinkling lights used as decoration at his birthday party (apparently, he'd had some other intention for them). She also didn't go nuts and leave him when he did crazy things like cut his very expensive dress pants off at the knees simply because he got tired of waiting for her in the hot sun. She came close to leaving once, when he wouldn't stop berating her for overstepping his idea of a wife's boundaries by publishing a book of her own in 1955, but she made him apologize and swear to never act that way again instead. Frank upheld his promise when she published another book a few years later. A wise choice, for who else knew him well enough to send precise instructions ahead to the president of an award ceremony to make sure Frank got his meal at the banquet prepared to the extreme specifications of a spoiled rockstar?[16] The fact was, Frank needed her, and they both knew it. She was the tether that held him together and kept him from drifting out of touch with reality and losing himself in his own mind.

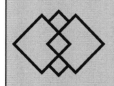

Fast Fact: The meal that Olgivanna sent instructions for when Frank was to receive a gold medal from the American Institute of Architects was one entirely plain piece of whitefish that was cooked over the fire (heaven forbid it should be cooked in or on the fire), one entirely plain baked potato, some peas, raspberry Jello, coffee, and exactly one quart of Grade A skimmed milk.[17]

Likewise, Frank was always there for her when it really counted. Cruel tragedy did not spare Olgivanna, just as it hadn't spared Frank. Her daughter from her first marriage, Svetlana, was pregnant in the fall of 1946. She was driving with her two boys, Brandoch (four) and Daniel (one and a half), when something made her lose control of the car. She had been suffering from fainting spells due to pregnancy, and many thought that might have been the cause, but little Brandoch later said that baby Daniel had started to fall out of the car and she'd grabbed for him, losing control of the wheel as they crossed over a bridge. The car went through the bridge railing and into the water, throwing four-year-old Brandoch free of the vehicle in the process, saving his life. The water wasn't very deep, but the mud beneath grabbed hold of the car. Brandoch got help from good Samaritans on the road, but by the time the car had been hauled out, it was too late. Baby Daniel had died on impact. Svetlana was still alive when they pulled her free, but she did not make it to the hospital.[18]

Olgivanna's sorrow was too great; she could no longer take charge, so Frank did. Not only did he serve as a source of comfort in such a terrible time, but he also took complete control of the funeral arrangements. He wouldn't allow the casket to be placed in their living room at the funeral because he knew that Olgivanna would never want to enter that room again. When she retreated into depression, refused to eat, and began living in a tent, it was Frank who coaxed her out of it.[19]

Odd as they both were, and prone to eyebrow-raising eccentricities and tempers, Frank had at last found a woman who fit him naturally, who complemented his creative traits and at the same time kept him humble … at least as humble as he could ever hope to make himself. Though they at times drove each other batty, they lifted each other up in times of trouble, and that is one of the surest signs of true love.

Last Days

Frank always held an Easter Sunday festival at Taliesin West, which was something like his Sunday picnics with the Lloyd Joneses all those years ago but with ten times the style. In 1959 over a hundred guests came to eat breakfast and celebrate, surrounded by bright bouquets of both flowers and painted Easter eggs. The Fellowship students sang hymns while the guests joined in.[20]

It was the end of March, and plans were already underway for a 92nd birthday party for Frank in June. However, Frank's son Lloyd informed him right around Easter that Kitty had died. To Lloyd's great surprise, Frank seemed very upset by the news, though he hadn't spoken to Kitty in years and had left her so callously for another woman. On April 4th, only ten days after hearing the news, Frank fell ill. He had pains in his abdomen and was rushed to the hospital. After a surgery to remove an obstruction, he seemed to get better. To everyone's shock, though, he died quite suddenly on April 9th, following his first love, the pretty redhead in the pink dress, into the next life.[21]

Sources

1 Huxtable, 2004.

2 Huxtable, 2004.

3 Huxtable, 2004.

4 Huxtable, 2004.

5 Huxtable, 2004.

6 Huxtable, 2004.

7 Huxtable, 2004.

8 Huxtable, 2004.

9 Huxtable, 2004.

10 Huxtable, 2004.

11 Huxtable, 2004.

12 Secrest, 1998.

13 Secrest, 1998.

14 Secrest, 1998.

15 Secrest, 1998.

16 Secrest, 1998.

17 Secrest, 1998.

18 Secrest, 1998.

19 Secrest, 1998.

20 Thorne-Thomsen, 2014.

21 Huxtable, 2004.

Chapter 10
Frank Lloyd Wright
Today

Frank spent 72 years working as an architect, and in that time he raised an incredible number of buildings up out of the earth. Many still stand today, speaking to his incredible craftsmanship and his ability to create futuristic designs. Many of his buildings, so bizarre in their own time, fit right in with the styles and fashions of today — probably because, as the widely hailed Father of American Architecture, many of the buildings of today are actually modeled after his designs. Any building will fall into disrepair if not kept up, but some of his more famous buildings have been updated and restored, such as Fallingwater — which you can actually pay to tour. Hollyhock House is an art school and museum that has been restored over the years by donations from the community. The Guggenheim Museum is still very much in use, though it continues to frustrate every curator who attempts to run it due to its slanting walls.

Sadly, other buildings were torn down shortly after they were built because their mastery and aesthetic was not yet appreciated or understood. The Larkin Building, for instance, created with such care for the comfort and safety of the workers within, was declared an eyesore by local critics and the city of Buffalo. It was demolished in 1950.[1] In other case, though the public loved Frank's work, financial issues took precedent over art. Thus, the stunning Midway Gardens, with its grand gardens and theaters and dance floors, was torn down during the Great Depression — with much sweat and backbreaking effort by those involved.

City officials and bankrupt businessmen could tear down some of Frank's buildings, but even after death, his work lived on, took up a life of its own, and was passed on to others.

A Lasting Legacy

Not even death could stop Frank from building. In 1956, he had been asked by the congregation of Annuciation Greek Orthodox church in Wauwatosa, Wisconsin to build them a new church. Though he died in 1959, having only designed the plans and never having seen a single brick laid, the building began to take shape in a Wisconsin field in 1960.[2]

People from neighborhoods around the site flocked to it, puzzled by the odd circular shape. The Space Age had started in the late '50s, so everyone knew what a spaceship was supposed to look like. That odd church, modeled after the famous domed Hagia Sophia cathedral in Istanbul, fit the bill of a spaceship.[3] Perhaps it would hover into the sky and leave crop circles in the field when it was completed.

The church was a huge domed circle set atop cross-shaped supports, like a flying saucer on a landing pad. A circular pool stood in front to reflect the church's alien image back at it. Inside, it was one perfectly open circular space free of any sort of obstruction to block the eye or interrupt the circle.[4]

The Annunciation Church was one last respectful nod from Frank to the future. Frank never looked back, and even after death, he was looking forward. He was born into the world during the time of horse-drawn buggies and left it with his eyes fixed on space with the rest of America. No matter his age, he always stayed current, being one of the first people to own a car and attaching himself to the greatest minds of his day. In his work, he was always ahead of the time, creating office buildings that functioned like well-oiled machines and houses that rejected the pomp of the Victorian style and instead served the functionality of American life, while still remaining beautiful and desirable. Only his fashion sense stayed in the past — or perhaps in some world of his own creation — with his mink collars, tweed jackets, flowing capes, twirling canes, and porkpie hats.[5]

He attracted imaginative clients, many of whom shared his larger-than-life personality and ego. The ordinary just wouldn't do; Frank drew the extraordinary to himself like a magnet. He worked for one of the pioneers of mail-order shopping, a car enthusiast, a stock market millionaire, an eccentric art collector, and creatives from around the world. However, Frank only ever really built for himself, and perhaps that's what made him so great. He understood that he had something special — an unmatched eye for architecture that allowed him to break old boundaries in brand new ways — and he didn't let anyone else's opinion stand in the way of his own creative force. True, he had his many faults in his personal life, but he loved deeply in his own ways. He paved the way for true American architecture and helped shape its unique identity. His open floor plans, ranch style homes, built-ins, and central fireplaces are still coveted in modern homes today. Until his influence ceases to remain present in American culture, Frank Lloyd Wright will continue to traverse the future.

Sources

1   Huxtable, 2004.

2   Thorne-Thomsen, 2014.

3   Thorne-Thomsen, 2014.

4   Thorne-Thomsen, 2014.

5   Huxtable, 2004.

Conclusion

The light from the home's one main window casts sunbeams over the small, slightly shabby home. A small boy named Frank sits at the table in front of the window, waiting for his mother. This little boy is not allowed the fancy sweets he covets in shop windows; he does not know the luxuries of the rich boys at his private school. What he doesn't yet know is that what he has is far greater. He has a mother driven to see him succeed, and the blocks and pegs she carries in her arms as she comes to join him at the table are the greatest gifts this particular boy could ever receive. These gifts from the revolutionary teacher, Froebel, will unlock something hidden inside Frank. A talent his mother already knows is there; she feels it in her blood when she looks at him.

Neither knows the tragedies that await him ... nor the great triumphs (though they are imagined). Neither knows that he will inherit many traits, both good and bad, from his father, the man they both will come to look on with disdain. Neither knows he will stumble many times in his pursuit of love and personal happiness, or that he will intertwine his life with a number of proud, intelligent women who will leave their marks on his life and his work.

What Frank's mother does know is that her boy has potential. What Frank knows, as he touches the wooden circles, cylinders, rectangles, and triangles, is that he has found something that delights him. From this moment on, he will pursue this feeling of creation — of molding shapes into beautiful forms. Potential amounts to little unless bestowed upon someone with the ambition, passion, and smallest tinge of madness needed to harness it into something that can help shape the world.

Author's Note

While preparing to buy our first home on a tight budget, my husband and I watched far too many episodes of a highly addictive home renovation show called *Fixer Upper*. After just a few episodes, I began to detect a pattern in what features people wanted in their homes. Everyone asked for open floor plans in the main living area, making the kitchen, den, and dining room span out into a single warm, inviting place. Lots of natural lighting in every room was a must. When given three options for which home to renovate, most people chose the one with an authentic fireplace in the living room. Women became giddy over bookshelves and storage spaces built right into the walls.

Many people want a house that looks somewhat like this in large part due to the influence of Frank Lloyd Wright.

Little did I know that all those features were pioneered by Frank Lloyd Wright in his never-ending romantic quest to keep American families close to the nature he loved so dearly. It makes sense; Earth is our true home, so it follows that the houses that mimic the wide open space of the natural world, that allow us to bathe in natural sunlight, and that blend into the landscape around them would feel the most "homey." Frank tapped into something deep within the human psyche when he designed his revolutionary prairie houses, and it's maddening to think that, like many geniuses before and after him, his work was not widely appreciated in his own time.

However, Frank didn't really need public opinion to validate his talents. Thanks to a doting mother and his natural ego, Frank was assured of his own genius at all times. With such charisma and genius often comes eccentricities, and Frank is no exception. Frank's oddities are what I love most about him. Architectural design is not something I particularly have an eye for (though I can appreciate it on many different levels), but great characters are, and Frank is one of the funniest, most maddening, and most oddly endearing characters I've ever come across. The best part? He was real.

As freeing and delightful as reading fiction is, you don't always have to turn to it for a great story. By opening a history book, you can find a man who wears his mother's mink collar around his neck, who cuts his fancy pants off at the knee because he's tired of waiting on his wife in the hot sun, and who can't resist using his borrowed bus fare on Japanese artwork and still have the gall to show up to the same lender asking for more money. You'll also find that that same strange man saved a crippled boy from bullies in his youth, saved thousands with his incredibly safe building designs in his prime, and throughout his career never forgot to include a special gift for the children who would dwell inside his homes.

Yes, he had his many faults, but underneath the all-too-human failures, extraordinary beauty and talent shone through him. Just like all of us, he had his moments of glory and his moments of shame (though perhaps both were on a larger scale than the average person's). It is humans that make history. Thus, if you want to truly understand human nature, you must dive headlong into the great stories of the past.

APPENDIX A
FAMILY TREE

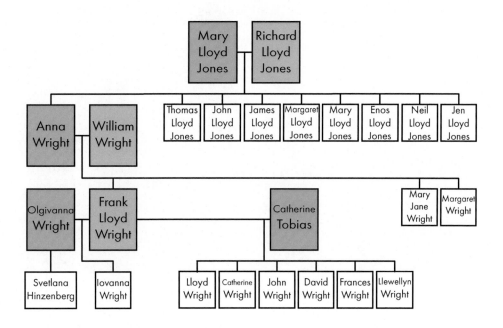

Appendix B
Guest Feature:
Meeting Frank Lloyd
Wright

—MORTON BALABAN

I graduated from the University of Illinois [with a degree] in architecture in 1956. And in about '52 or '53, Wright came to present his mile-high building at the Chicago Public Library. I was there. Wright came in his

1946 black Lincoln Continental, with a black frock, and a porkpie hat, and his silver-headed cane. He came into the studio and hopped up on the desk, and we just sat at his feet like children at the feet of the gods. He was an arrogant son of a [expletive], but we all allow for that. Da Vinci was probably a jerk, too, but we allow for genius. Frank Lloyd Wright was the genius of American architecture. There hasn't been anything like him before or since.

I was 20 when I met him, and he was around 86. He was an old man, but he was full of energy and vitality. I remember when someone commented that he was talking a lot about himself — which was kind of a gutsy thing to say to the Liebermeister — Wright said, "Early in life, I had to decide between hypocritical humility and honest arrogance. I chose honest arrogance, and I've never been sorry." He was arrogant, and he had reason to be arrogant.

But we wanted him to talk about his structures, so he was explaining to us young architects the concept of the root of the mile-high building. In other words, the building had a long shaft going into the earth bound to bedrock, which in Chicago is roughly 150 feet down. And that's what the structure would sit on, the bedrock on a 150-foot pier. The building would then blossom out like a tree with branches. The concept was again embedded in nature, all of which he was an advocate of — of organic colors and making the architecture part of the landscape. And his idea, which flew in the face of what he was doing in the Prairie House, was that he could build a building with hundreds of hundreds of apartments in it, probably thousands, and have an open space all around it. So, as he said, the building would cast a shadow of itself on the ground, rather than have a whole crowd of buildings. Instead, there'd be no buildings around it. Like a tree, it could cast its shadow on the ground.

We loved that idea and loved the concept. Although, honestly, young architects in the '50s and '60s were not much following Wright's principles. Mies van der Rohe made it easy for us. He called Wright the greatest architect of the 19th century, which was kind of a jab because we were all in the 20th century.

Wright's greatest Prairie Houses were built between 1895 and 1907, when he was doing those great houses in Oak Park, a suburb of Chicago. As he moved on into other phases of his life, he went into other phases of his architecture. David [and Gladys] Wright's house in Phoenix is a series of circles. Obviously, the Guggenheim was a series of interlocking round structures completely unlike his Prairie style. He kept reinventing himself. In the '60s and '70s, he had practically no clients. He was a well-known lousy businessman. He had a lot of women and cars and a lifestyle that he really couldn't afford to be in.

But meeting him one on one was a treat. It was 60 years ago, and I remember it like it was yesterday because it really had an impact. It had an impact on all of us, all of us young architects, but we did not try to copy his architecture. Those who did only knew his vocabulary — so we would write prose while he was writing poetry. Nobody has really been able to capture his architecture.

Wright literally invented the modern high-rise, but his only high-rise was Price Tower in Oklahoma. That was not his forte. His forte was residential. Everybody knows the story about Hib Johnson of Johnson Wax, and Johnson calling Wright from his house, Wingspread, in Racine, Wisconsin, saying: "I'm having a dinner party with very important guests, and it's raining on my head." And Wright says to him, "So, move your chair."

When Wright was invited as a guest to people's houses that he had designed, like famously in Grand Rapids where he stayed overnight, when they got up in the morning, he had completely rearranged all the furniture, because he didn't like the way they had arranged it.

Frank Lloyd Wright's Influence

I am an architect practicing in the Chicago area, and I've designed probably 30-40 Prairie School structures. I've taught it to my daughters, and my daughters have taught it to schoolchildren. I was an artist-in-residence at a grade school, and as a project I built a Prairie House playhouse in the parking lot with about 100 kids from the art classes, their parents, and a couple of my sub-contractors. So, some day, maybe 10 or 15 years from now, people will be telling their architect, "I want it more Prairie, I want more colors of the landscape, more horizontality." Today, when you see a structure being built in a Prairie style, people think it's modern; and actually the style of architecture is a hundred years old. Good design doesn't get old.

Home built by architect Morton S. Balaban; Wilmette, IL

Wright was a remarkable talent. (I would say he was my biggest influence.) I have done houses that I think he would be pleased with. And people who own some of these houses have asked me, when they were furnishing, to please come and pass judgment on their furniture and lighting fixtures. So, yeah, Wright had influence on people. [Many people are familiar with] the Hollyhock House and the houses of Southern California, but his great genius was the Midwestern Prairie House — from Spring Green to Oak Park. He had a great influence on many architects who have lived 30-40 years past him. And I think his architecture will always be here. History books are filled with it, and there are still architects trying to emulate it — me being one of them.

I have found, like Wright found, that his designs would not be faithfully reproduced from his drawings unless he was involved in the construction. Unfortunately, he never did get the idea that the money was not in being the architect. The money was in being the contractor. He would be the supervising architect, but he would hire general contractors to build his buildings for the clients, but unless the sub-contractors are in your employ, you don't get the exact detail that you want. God lives in the details. And there are details that are extremely important that the everyday client doesn't know or doesn't realize. And if the architect is there every day, he makes sure that those details are executed.

Why You Should Care About Wright

Frank Lloyd Wright embodied a timeless architecture. As he said, "Architecture is frozen music." These are not things that are done for a day, a week, a month, or a year. They're for 100 years. So, first of all, if you wish to be immortal, this is the one way for immortality. If you leave structures, it's a sign that you've been here. And it's a marriage of art and engineering. Although Wright was an engineer who was not very well educated in his engineering and pushed the envelope always too far so that he had semi-failures — or certainly things that leaked, and that bent, and deflected — but he didn't care. What he was worried about was the timelessness of the architecture and its beauty. The architecture we're doing today will be dated. His work is never dated. One hundred years from now, his work will still be considered contemporary — a word which means "of the day," and yet he will be contemporary 200 years from now. Now *that* is having made a mark on civilization.

So, why should they care? That's a good reason to care.

You've been here.

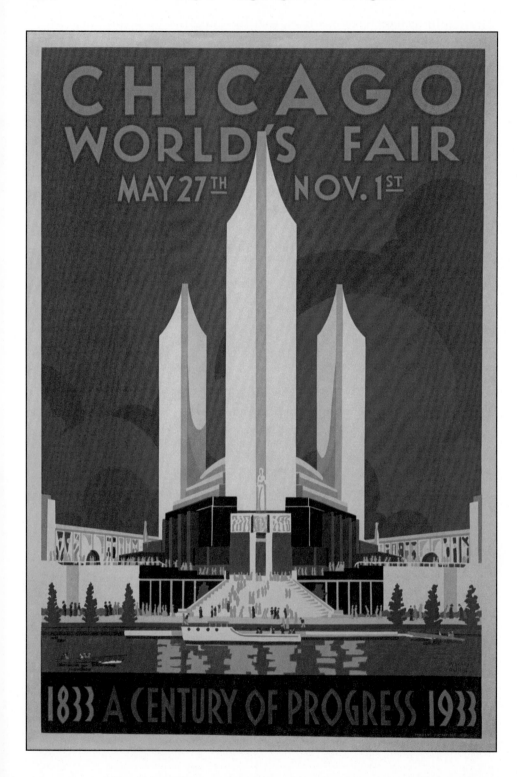

GLOSSARY

Age of Enlightenment: a movement started in the early 18th century that put much emphasis on scientific discovery and thinking. Religion, politics, social issues, and economic debates were approached with rational and scientific reasoning.

Cable Car: a type of transportation where trolleys on rails are pulled by cables running at a constant, consistent speed.

California Romanza: Frank's own term for the building style of the Hollyhock House.

Cantilevering/cantilever: a beam or plank that juts out over open space, held up only by support on one end is called a cantilever. Cantilevering is the technique Frank used to make Fallingwater. Each level jutted (or cantilevered) out from the core stone column of the home at a different angle.

Chambered nautilus shell: a spiraled shell with a hollow space inside, usually for a creature to live in, like a garden snail.

Concrete piers: concrete blocks set into the ground to support a building's foundation.

Crystallography: the study of the shapes that atoms make inside crystal formations.

Deed: a written legal document that proves ownership of something, usually a piece of property like a house.

Draftsman: someone who draws up detailed, technical plans for a structure, such as machines, electronics, or buildings. Frank started his architectural career as a draftsman for Silsbee & Corwin.

Druid priest: the druids were an ancient class of people in Wales and Ireland. They were educated, upper-class people who served as poets, philosophers, artists, and priests.

Druid religion: the druids did not leave many artifacts or writings behind, so not much is known of their religion except what is gleaned through the Romans and Greeks. The druid religion was a pagan one believed to include human sacrifice. They put strong emphasis on nature and the elements, with oak trees and mistletoe featured heavily in their rituals and symbolism.

Floating foundations: reinforced concrete slabs that float on top of loose soil, moving along it as it compacts and loosens under extreme temperatures and circumstances, rather than cracking or crumbling.

Gingerbread Houses: edible houses made of baked goods, the slightly spicy gingerbread foremost among them.

Hearth: the floor of the fireplace that extends out in front of it.

Hexagonal: constructed in the six-sided shape of a hexagon.

Idyllic: something (usually a time or place) that is picturesque or evokes extreme happiness.

Inglenook: a small recessed room around a fireplace

Liebermeister: this title means "beloved teacher" in German. Frank referred to Louis Sullivan as his Liebermeister.

Masonry: stone work.

Mediums: people who serve as a channel to the spirit world, talking to ghosts and delivering their messages to the living.

Mesa: a landform that looks much like a tabletop, with a flat top and steep sides. Most commonly found in the southwest.

Mirror Imagery: when one thing is copied perfectly but reversed around an intervening axis or plane.

Modernist/ modernism:	the modernist movement arose in the late 19th century, and it rejected the ornate sentimentalism of the romantic era and praised the simple, sleek, and analytical. Its influence touched all areas of art, but for architecture it meant simplistic almost minimalistic designs for homes (made with the latest materials) instead of the highly decorative styles of the Victorian architecture that was previously popular.
Non-Objective Art:	an artistic style that created extremely abstract forms that the viewer couldn't associate with any known object. The hope was that with no comparisons between reality and the art, the viewer's mind could break away the barrier between our world and transcendental harmony with the universe.
Organic Architecture:	Frank Lloyd Wright's term for his own work and the inspiration for prairie houses. The idea was to let the lay of the land dictate the structure and design of the building instead of forcing the land to fit a prefabricated vision for the building.
Organic Whole Architecture:	a stylistic concept meaning that the parts of a building come together seamlessly and naturally to create beauty and harmony. Frank's mentor, Louis Sullivan, applied this concept to his work and taught it to Frank.

Prairie House: perhaps Frank's most iconic style, these buildings put Frank on the architectural map with their open floorplans, natural coloring and decoration, banded windows, and lack of attics or basements.

Quintessential: the ultimate example of something; an adjective that indicates the best representation of the most typical or perfect form of something.

Radiant heating: heating a home through heat sources embedded in the walls, floor, or ceiling. Radiant heating systems can rely on a hot air source, an electric source, or a hot water source. For Frank's first Usonian home, he ran hot water pipes through the floors to generate heat that would rise up and fill the rooms.

Romantics: members of a school of thought that developed in arts and literature in the late 18th century. Romantics believed in focusing on individual sentiment, inspiration, and subjectivity rather than adhering to the strict logical, objective thinking of the era which came before, the Age of Enlightenment.

Shingle Style: a style of architecture in which shingles are not merely designated to roofs, but placed all around the exterior of the home, creating a simplistic but eye-catching result. Frank learned this style from J. L. Silsbee and used it on his own home in Oak Park.

Snobbyists and Goodyites: these were Frank's personal nicknames for the rich children who went to the private school he attended early in life.

Space Age: the start of this era was marked by the Russian launch of the first satellite, Sputnik 1, on October 4th, 1957. In a panicked rush to catch up to the technology of the Russians, the American government began to put heavy emphasis on math and science, and society began to dream of adventures in unexplored space.

Spinster: a woman who is past the typical age for marriage and considered unlikely to ever marry. The general age of spinsterhood keeps getting pushed back farther as the years go by. In the 1800s, a girl of just 18 might be approaching spinsterhood. Now the general age for the term is around 40.

Sublime: something so grand, beautiful, or excellent that it inspires awe.

Sunlights and moonlights: lights meant to mimic the light of the sun and moon respectively.

Textile block: a concrete block cast into an unusual or beautiful pattern. Frank built four famous homes out of textile blocks.

Textiles: a woven fabric that is knitted, crocheted, knotted, or felted into a pattern.

The Chicago School: an architectural style in which the architects displayed the new, innovative steel frames used for construction, keeping the buildings the same simplistic, skyward-reaching shape of the frames themselves. The style lead to the creation of the first skyscrapers. Some architects who were part of the Chicago School include William Le Baron Jenney, Daniel Burnham, and Louis Sullivan.

Tracer: the entry-level version of a draftsman. Instead of drawing up the full plans, tracers make minor technical adjustments to the senior and junior draftsman's work if needed and then trace all of the details onto a final sheet that is used for construction.

Transcendentalists: followers of transcendentalism, which was a branch of romanticism that adhered to the belief that man could connect to the divinity within himself by becoming one with nature.

Transportation Building: Louis Sullivan's entry into the 1893 Chicago World's Fair. It was a public building meant for housing large means of transportation like trains and ocean liners.

Trilingual: someone who speaks three languages. In addition to English, Mamah Cheney knew French and German, and even later learned Swedish.

Usonian style: a style pioneered by Frank Lloyd Wright to create affordable, safe, and beautiful homes for the common man. The style is characterized by long, one-floor designs. Usonian homes are now known as American ranch homes.

Utopian: modeled after or seeking absolute perfection.

Timeline

June 8, 1867:	Frank is born
1876:	Centennial Exposition, Anna brings home Froebel gifts
1878:	Frank goes to Lloyd Jones farm
1885:	William leaves
1886:	Frank briefly attends the University of Wisconsin
1887:	Frank arrives in Chicago
June 1, 1889:	Frank marries Kitty
1893:	Chicago World's Fair, Frank leaves Adler & Sullivan to start own business, builds playroom for his children
1898:	Frank builds his studio
1901:	Frank's Prairie House design appears in the *Ladies' Home Journal*
1902:	Heurtley House is built
1904:	The Larkin Administration Building and the Cheney House

1905:	Frank's first trip to Japan, Unity Temple commissioned
1908:	The Robie House commissioned, Unity Temple completed
1909:	Frank leaves for Germany to work for Ernst Wasmuth with Mamah Cheney in tow
1910:	Frank returns home to Kitty, Robie House finished
1911:	Frank builds Taliesin
1914:	Midway Gardens commissioned
August 15, 1914:	Taliesin murders
1916:	Imperial Hotel officially commissioned
1918:	Frank moves to Japan to build the Imperial Hotel
1921:	Hollyhock House is completed
1922:	Imperial Hotel completed, and Kitty divorces Frank
1923:	Anna Lloyd Jones dies, Miriam and Frank marry
1927:	The State of California accepts the Hollyhock House from Aline Barnsdall
1928:	Frank marries Olgivanna
1929:	The Great Depression starts, Midway Gardens torn down after much effort
1936:	Frank builds first Usonian home for the Jacobs family, Fallingwater construction begins

1937:   Taliesin West is built

1939:   World War II begins, Fallingwater completed

1956:   Construction begins on Guggenheim Museum, Price Company Tower unveiled

1957:   Marion Country Civic Center built; Russia launches Sputnik 1, harkening the Space Age

1959:   The Guggenheim Museum officially opens, Frank dies April 9th

1960:   Annunciation Church begins construction

BIBLIOGRAPHY

Balaban, Morton. "Frank Lloyd Wright." Telephone interview. 1 Sept. 2016.

Huxtable, Ada Louise. *Frank Lloyd Wright: A Life.* New York: Lipper/ Penguin, 2004.

Secrest, Meryle. *Frank Lloyd Wright: A Biography.* Chicago: The University of Chicago Press, 1998.

Thorne-Thomsen, Kathleen. *Frank Lloyd Wright for Kids.* Chicago: Chicago Review Press, 2014.

Wright, Frank Lloyd. *Frank Lloyd Wright: An Autobiography.* New York: Horizon Press, 1977.

İПDEX

About the Author

Hannah Sandoval became a freelance writer and editor straight out of college with a BA in English from the University of Tennessee at Chattanooga in tow. In May of 2016, she launched her own manuscript editing and ghostwriting business, PurpleInkPen, at the age of twenty-three. She has worked on over a dozen manuscripts, either as a writer or copy editor. In the summer of 2016, she earned a professional book editor certification from IAP Career College to further her knowledge of the publishing world.

Hannah lives in Chattanooga, TN, with her husband, Stephen, and a rambunctious corgi named Vanellope who has more sass than Hannah could ever hope to have. Hannah's first novel, Arcamira – an epic fantasy/paranormal crossover initially written at the age of fourteen – is being reworked and published in biweekly installments on the serialized literature website, Channillo. Hannah also writes weekly for her blog on breaking into the freelance world. The blog, I Just Want to Write, discusses both how she has found success and the mistakes she's made along the way.

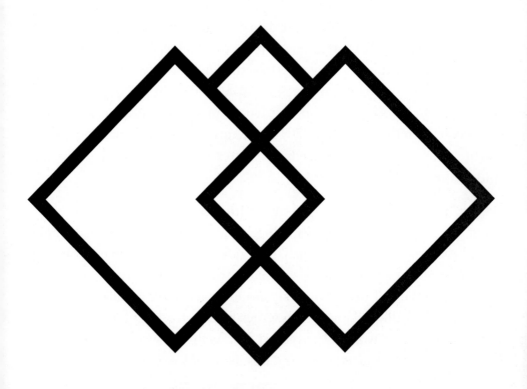